BOG ALL AB

By **J**

THE THIRD AND LAST 'SWEAR' BOOK

£1.30
0/22

xx

ACKNOWLEDGEMENTS

COVER PHOTO: The Old General Pub, Hyson Green Nottingham
Trevor Bartlett – Nottingham Evening Post

I originally wrote 'Yo'd Mek A Parson Swear' as a family history for my children never believing it could be of interest to anyone other than my family. It was only when Alan Bailey (retired producer and sound engineer) saw it and thought it 'brilliant' (his word, not mine) that I gave any serious consideration to publishing it. But for him, it would still be a ragged and unfinished document languishing on my PC. His idea's and art work have been a revelation and I would like to thank him for his unstilted patient help and the graphic work he's done on what is after all, a lot of ancient uncared for, ergo dog eared photo's that I think have given additional interest to all three books.

I would also like to thank the many and in some cases, unknown Nottingham people who have contacted me via my email address and encouraged me to continue writing. People like Steven Henson, Mo Francis, Di Edwards and her lovely mum Pat whom I surprised with a birthday visit, Carol Lawson and her mum Audrey who also got a birthday visit, Patsy Newman to whom I have once again become quite close, Gwen Brett, Diane Hornby, Marjorie Nelson, George Saxton, Margaret Willetts(as was!) all of whom I have recently rekindled my friendship with.

My thanks also go to the Army Records Office, Bury St Edmunds in Suffolk.
Readers of my two previous books will have learned I never knew my Father in spite of a lifelong search. The search continues and so far Army Records have come up with this: - L/Cpl C Lowther late of the Suffolk Regiment. From our Service Registers I was able to ascertain that Cecil Lowther joined the Suffolk Regiment on 2nd August 1939 Army number 5825135 for a 5/7 term. He was transferred to the RASC on 12th December 1941. Previously he was a Trolley bus Conductor for Ipswich Council.

Thanks also to Julia Knott who, having read my book and sympathising with my lack of knowledge about my Father set out to help me. Sixteen years of maintenance led me to imagine there would be a thick file and all that had been found were just two ancient yellowed, tissue thin pages of an original High Court order dated 30.12.1941 in which mam had been awarded 2s/6d (little over 12p today!!) and a further variation order dated 6.1.1947 which increased it to ten bob (50p).

OTHER WORKS BY THE SAME AUTHOR:

'Yo'd Mek A Parson Swear'   Dec 2008
'Yo'd Mek A Parson Swear....Again! June 2009

FOREWORD

Oh wow, its 70yrs since the outbreak of World War 2 and people's memories are being stirred yet again. Back then I was a mere twelve days off being born. It must have been a bad time for my mother to be carrying me, not knowing what was to come and whether she would live to see another day. Maybe she was worried sick and that's why she passed me over to her sister in Birmingham to bring up. I don't know and it's far too late for me to ask about it or worry now. All I know for sure is that at three years of age, I was reunited with my mother and was bought to Nottingham to join a ready made family of a 'father' 'brother' and 'sister'.

As kids growing up in war torn Britain in those days we, like a lot of families, were dreadfully deprived of most of the stuff usually associated with childhood and taken for granted by today's children. Back then and in far too many cases even the most basic human needs like decent food, warm clothes, shoes and toys were few and far between and in school we barely had exercise books and pencils let alone the likes of calculators. We learned maths not through books but by chanting tables which we had to learn off by heart and we were taught *mental* arithmetic. To drill the figures home, the teacher used a foot long wooden Imperial ruler...straight across the backs of our knuckles.

There were no fridges – ergo no such thing as sell by dates to worry us. Our parents simply applied the age old tried and tested 'use your nose and common sense' method to determine whether food was good to eat or not and believe me, we didn't need Mrs Edwina Curry to tell us an egg was *bad*! And yet, for all that, I don't recall too much if anything in the way of food poisoning, mind that could well have had more to do with the fact there was not much food to be had in the first place so it didn't last long enough to go bad! Rationing was fair but minuscule by today's standards and the following is a typical week's allowance;

Bacon and ham: A miserly 4oz, easily gobbled up in one sandwich!

Meat: This was whatever was available to the value of 1s.2d (6p today). Sausages were not rationed but could be very difficult to find and although offal (liver, lights, kidneys brains and tripe etc) was not initially rationed, as the war wore on and things got really tight, they also formed part of the meat allowance. It was a good idea to flatter your local butcher as he had his favourites and anything that came in was doled out to them first. You might very well have wanted roast leg of lamb for Sunday dinner, but if scrag end was all they had....

Cheese: A miserable 2oz, easily swallowed in one mouthful! But this did yo-yo weekly and eventually went up to 4oz and towards the end of the war, even up to 8oz.

Margarine: 4oz. This near impossible to spread dubious product resembled a bright Lego yellow axle grease block and tasted roughly, with the accent on *rough,* the same too. We King kids preferred to put lard, brown sauce, condensed milk, tomato puree or even sugar on our bread

4

if mam wasn't looking! Oddly, due to the additives in that stuff, it made sure we were all a damn sight healthier than today's kids.

Butter: 2oz. But this almost holy grail of delicacies was strictly reserved for our parents!

Milk: 3 pints, though occasionally dropping to 2. A dried version was available at the rate of 1 packet per four weeks but we kids did get a daily half pint of milk in schools, originally paying a penny bottle for it but later it was given free. Apart from that, generally speaking the only milk we kids had at home was the tinned condensed stuff and we had it on bread in place of jam and also watered down it became part of our evening meal of 'pobs'; chunks of stale bread soaked in this sweet milky gravy. Only now, at this late date, do I stop to wonder how in the absence of fridges or larders, they managed to keep their food and especially their milk fresh?

Sugar: 8oz per person but again this was reserved for my parents and we had to use saccharin. Ugh!

Jam: A 1lb jar every two months and when it was empty, trust me it was wiped clean, small hands easily getting right inside the jar to extract every last precious jewel coloured morsel.

Tea: 2oz. Hence the strong and never to be forgotten aroma of stewed tea in every kitchen as each housewife boiled that last bit of colour out of the leaves.

Eggs:	1 fresh egg a week if available but often only one every two weeks. Dried egg 1 packet every four weeks but again we King kids never saw an egg and when we finally got our first boiled one we didn't know what to do with it.
Sweets:	12oz every four weeks, so now you know why we ate those awful alternatives. This ration was not to be repealed until February the 5th 1953 seven years *after* the end of the war.

We somehow managed perfectly well on what now looks in retrospect to be a very limited and meagre diet and it's only after looking through the above list I now realise why the adults of my childhood bought everything by the ounce long after the war was over! It's obvious isn't it? After all those years of war, it had become a habit to think and buy in such small amounts and it was only the advent of the supermarkets and the convenience of pre-packaging that changed all that.

We also manage to live without PC's or TV's and that was not *just* because we were desperately poor although we were, it was because most of these things had barely, if at all, been invented. We were proud to wear a school uniform back then and mostly they were 'hand me down' hand me downs from sister to brother, brother to sister, neighbour to neighbour so they were far from new.

That it was uniform in colour, patched if necessary and reasonably clean was all that mattered and often these were the only 'good' clothes we had to our names. If there was a gap of several years between brothers for example, any trousers passed down to the smallest would be chopped off at the knees, the waist band hoisted by strong elastic braces up under the armpits placing the buttoned 'flies' incongruously in the middle of the wearers chest!

We were scared of everything and everybody. What could be scary about Mickey Mouse? The gas mask made in the cartoon characters image that's what. I can remember vividly the utter terror, the horrid rubbery smell and the sheer claustrophobia of having that awful thing strapped firmly onto my head and no amount of encouragement, cajoling or even threats could stop the panic rising in my young throat.

You would think that since there had never been a time in our young lives when we hadn't had the cacophonous lullaby of a mournful air raid siren nightly turning the very blood in our veins to sheer ice, we would have got used to it, but I for one, never did. Even unto today, just hearing that sound in a film or as a reminder of the war brings me out in goose bumps. I also held a special hatred and fear for the nasty smelly concrete box called an air raid shelter at the bottom of Moffat Street into which at times we were ushered by our terrified parents and neighbours.

Lit only by torches it eerily turned adult faces into nightmarish caricatures of what were ordinarily the familiar countenances of our friendly neighbours and family. And although I lived in constant fear of the ghosts that hid in the yawning blackness under the double bed and in the dark corners of the unlit attic in which we huddled together like sardines against the cold - often several to a bed - when that siren went off in the night, we had been taught to dive *under* it unceremoniously scattering the ghosts, mice droppings and dust as we did so, the fear of one greatly outweighing the fear of the other.

We were frightened to death of things that walked and skittered in the night, mainly bedbugs and mice! Teachers and coppers terrified us and we knew only too well even minor transgressions warranted a painful clip around the ear (or more colloquially, a 'bat round the tab'!) but we were even more scared if the teacher or policeman went home and told our parents what we had been up to for that meant second and often even harsher punishment.

Even some words struck the fear of God into us; words like 'cellar', 'Hitler', 'cane', 'wet bed', but the oft heard phrase 'just wait'll yer dad gets home' never applied to us since our dad was in comparison to mam, a pussy cat. She had little or more usually no patience whatsoever, so waiting for dad was not an option and by the time he got home, the punishment would have already been meted out and we'd be wearing our bruises for the next ten days or more, in or out of school depending on the severity of the beating and the means by which it had been ministered, usually whatever was nearest to hand, her aim being deadly. In later years when she came home proudly bearing a silver rose bowl she had won, I was not at all surprised.   She   had   won   it   for   her   skill   at throwing....darts! (She later gave it to me and I still have it.)

Our manners were and do remain impeccable compared to today's youth. In our day not one child would be permitted to sit whilst an adult stood and no mam worth her salt would let her small child occupy a seat and would haul the said child onto her lap. It was automatic for kids to give up their seats and offering to carry heavy shopping bags for older people was second nature to us. Yet only today on a crowded bus trip into town I saw a young man in his 20's who was seated. A young woman got on with two small children and a baby in a pushchair. She placed the pushchair alongside the seated man and stood in front as the children valiantly clung to her legs for the entire journey. A few stops further on, a lady with a guide dog fumbled her way onto the bus. He was totally oblivious and never moved. It was not that lad's fault it was the fault of his upbringing. Good manners don't happen, they are taught and boy, were we ever taught and taught good. In our day there was common agreement between parents and teachers as to how to bring up the kids, the two governing bodies were not at war....and the unwritten understanding being we were to do as we were told and we did it without question.

Our polite concept of queuing has also been challenged as the folk patiently waiting for the Colwick car boot to open on a Sunday morning will testify. At the appointed gate opening minute, there is an en masse surge as strangers to our shores rush forwards on an every man for himself basis, much to the queues chagrin and many an angry exchange has taken place. This is not bad manners I hasten to add, it's merely their culture so we can't be too hard on them. But lately I noticed they are catching on to our ways and the older émigré's now stand in line along with the rest of us and complain just as vociferously when the new arrivals push in!

Glossary;

The Nottingham lingo as I knew it as a kid is all but dead and gone. We no longer drink 'water', its now 'wart'a', we don't 'ask' anymore, we 'axe' and we drop the 'g' and add a 'k' to the endings of words like 'anything' and it comes out of the mouth of even some BBC presenters as 'anyfink'. There has been, over the last 25 years or so a shift to an almost sub gangsta language that in some instances only the kids can understand. In our teenage day we too used such words as 'dig it' and phrases like 'hot diggety dog'. Don't ask, I didn't know what it meant when I used it as a bona fide fully paid up member of the teenage sect and I sure as hell still don't know what it means now and I am sure the kids of today would find that terribly amusing.

So we too find fun in some of the things the kids today say; 'do you know where I'm coming from(????)', 'basically', 'at the end of the day', 'do you know what I'm saying?', 'wassuup? etc. So forgive me for including this recently updated version of our rich Nottingham accent yet again. After all, how do I know you are not an American tourist who suddenly gets home and finds he or she cannot understand some of the conversations in this tome? Thanks to all those of you who have emailed me and reminded me of more words and I would be grateful for any more I may have missed out.

Annall	Also.
Allus	Always
Annit	Hasn't it?
Atta	Have to.
Ahdo	Traditional greeting
Ayup	ditto
Ast	Ask.
Badleh	Ill.
Barmeh	Daft
Bat	Hit.
Batchy	Daft.
Battin' on	Moving fast.
Be said	No more arguing.
Blortin'	Crying.
Bobbar	Don't touch!
Boozer	Hostelry, pub.
Bostin'	In dire need of the loo.
Boz	Crossed, as in cross eyed.
Bunce	Illicit payment.
Bung 'ole	Cheese.
Cadge	Borrow.
Cadger	Incessant borrower.
Charlie	Ladies underskirt.
Charlie's dead	A glimpse of the above.
Chelp	Answer back in a cheeky way.
Chunter	Mutter under one's breath.
Cob	Bread roll.
Coggin	Apple core.
Corsey	Pavement.
Cowd	Cold.
Dab in	To get a move on.
Dannies	Baby's hands.

Dicks	Head lice.
Dinnit	Didn't it?
Dintah	Didn't I?
Dollally	Daft, simple.
Duck	A term of affection used by both sexes to both sexes.
Duddoo's	Sweeties.
Dunk	Dip ones biscuit in one's tea.
Enntit	Hasn't it.
Essa	Ever so.
Etta	Have to.
Eyya	Have you?
Eyyabindahn?	Have you been t'ut football match?
Eyyagorra?	Do you have?
Eyya gorrowt	Have you got anything?
Faunt	Found.
FizZoeeg	Face.
Frit	Afraid.
Frock	Dress.
Gawpin'	Staring at.
Gerr'off	Get off.
Gleg	Look at in a nosey fashion.
Gormy	A bit slow on the uptake.
Gorra	Got a.
Goyin' or gooin'	Going.
Gret	Great.
Guz	Goes.
Guzzunder	Commode or under-bed pot.
Hoity-toity	To think oneself better than.
Innit	Isn't it?
Inntit	As above.
Jitteh	Alleyway leading to

	back of terrace.
Ligger	Liar.
Lippy	Too quick to answer back, cheeky.
Lug holes	Ears.
Lugs	Knots in the hair.
Lummox	Buffoon.
Mardeh	Cowardly.
Mashin'	Brewing tea.
Missen	Myself.
Munt	Must not.
Nats piss	Weak tea.
Nesh	Someone who is always cold.
Nowt	Nothing.
Nunnoo's	Money given to children.
Owd	Old or hold.
Owja sweat	Take it easy.
Owt	Anything.
Oyya	Are you?
Oyya-beya-sen	Are you alone?
Pobs	Stale bread soaked in tea.
Poddle	To amble.
Pods	Baby's footwear, usually knitted.
Puddled	Mis-guided thinker, even daft.
Puther	Ooze out.
Rammel	Worthless rubbish.
Rawk	Tear through (say) hair with no thought as to pain only gain – mam's not mine!
Scrat	Anything meagre spread on bread.

Scrike	Cry.
Serry	Pal, mate, friend.
Shintin	She isn't at home
Shunta	Shouldn't have.
Sludgebump	Person greatly put upon by others.
Snap	Packed lunch.
Snided	Many of; as in snided with ants.
Splodge	To kiss.
Swiggin'	Drinking.
Swing fo' ya	Someone is in serious trouble.
Tab	Ear
Tinna or tint	It is not.
Towd	Told.
Tuffees	Sweets, oddly coffee was pronounced correctly.
Twist	Spoons of tea twisted up in newspaper.
Wantit or wannit	Wasn't it?
WazZoeeck	Idiot, loony, soft in the head.
Wesh	Wash.
Whittle	Worry unduly.
Wiggin'	Usually applied to kids listening into adult conversation.
Yerssen	Yourself.
Yent	You have not.
Yev or yav	You have.

Back in the forties and fifties, there were also some odd sayings that were peculiar to Nottingham. For example; 'Gi' ovva scrikin' yer mardy cah, else ah'll giyya summat ter scrike for'.

This meant 'Stop crying you coward or else I will give you something to cry for.' And was usually followed by a hard slap, this action rather defeating the purpose since the slapped one scriked anew and louder still!

Any word ending in 'Y' is pronounced 'eh' as the e in dead, e.g; jitteh (jitty), badleh (badly), mardeh (mardy) 'appeh (happy). Finally; if there are two words that *exactly* define the Nottingham twang its 'Gerr'off' (get off). To truly say it as it's colloquially said in these parts, you have to sound hyphenate the 'Gerr' from the 'off'. So say it thus; Gerro' - phf.

Now let's have a bit of a practice; say the following sentence. "Garrauntonnit an' gerro'phf, else ah'll bat yer tab ya gret lummox."

Now repeat it out loud a couple of times and that's it!! That's it, yo've gorrit, yo' talkin' proper Nottingham nah serry....

CHAPTER 1

BRIDE AND GROOM.

So, where was I? Oh yes, I remember, I'd been caught up in a wedding, my own. The date was April 2nd 1960. At just short of my 21st birthday I was now Mrs John Blacknell, a Sadie Sadie married lady, half of a couple or 'two hearts beating as one' as the romantics would have it, or as I preferred, a bride. In that one move I had gone from a Miss with, if I had but known it, the whole world at my fingertips, into a Mrs who suddenly had to grow up and grow up fast. *A bride?* Bah humbug, what was so special about being a bride anyway?

One day I was single, the next I took my dad's arm, walked with him down the aisle of St Stephens church on Bobbers Mill Road Nottingham, packed with all our family, friends and 'the lads', wearing a long white frock and carrying an armful of red roses (me not the lads!) I nervously said yes to the salient and few ancient words that were chanted over us, signed my old name for the last time in a big ledger and in the doing, I was hitched. Then everything changed and yet nothing changed except my name, address oh and my work load doubled!

Aren't brides supposed to be revered? I know in the absence of any parental help I'd barely had enough money for my part of the responsibilities of a half decent wedding – even the flowers carried by the bridesmaids were merely plastic daffodils given away free with soap powder and hand fashioned by me into passable posies with the addition of a few ribbons – they looked the part on the day but didn't stand up too well in the scent category – mind, they outlasted my bouquet! But I couldn't help but wonder why my beloved didn't revere his bride enough to have found a little something for a honeymoon no matter how brief? He managed to find enough money to go on 'the lad's' boozy autumn weekend to Blackpool that and every single year afterwards, marriage and finances not withstanding.

Once I had got back to Nottingham from my three year stay in Birmingham, I had fitted back in with my family as if I had never been away. I got a job at John Beal's on Peveril Street but was still expected and *did* tip up my wages unopened as before but mam said that because I was getting married, she would double my pocket money to £1 a week! Ahh, bless. Apart from running a rusty old dolls pram over the train of my wedding dress stored in a floor to ceiling cupboard in the attic I shared with Eileen and the continued threat to withdraw her consent to my marriage at the very last minute and make me wait until I was 21 - the then legal age of consent – mam left me pretty much alone and I had only my coming big day to worry about.

On that first day of our marriage we opened and took stock of the many wedding presents we had received. Everyone had been very generous with their gifts and we had an ironing board, various (then) innovative Pyrex glass cookware and a Pyrex rolling pin (still have and use it!), a red state of the art metal lamp came from Dereck Smith, Nobby and Pam had given us a handsome pair of bone handled meat carvers, Brenda and David a beautiful set of Poole pottery (I wish I STILL had that!), a handsome hearthrug came from Clac and Sheila, an expensive set of EPNS cutlery from Johns workplace Metallifacture, two

17

Whitney blankets - with satin edges - from his parents, a white candlewick bedspread from his Barrington (Cambs) based sister, a pair of the prettiest green pillow cases from Dot and Donny which I STILL have, an elegant table cloth and napkin set from Heather and Cyril, a pair of single sheets (?) came from the Duchess, a set of blue embroidered 'His and Hers' towels from Doris and Jeff, as well as various sets of towels and yet more pillow slips from my own workmates in Birmingham and finally, unbelievably fourteen pairs of double sheets from family and friends. Anybody would think somebody wet the bed! Anybody would be right and out of the two of us, only I knew that it wasn't my husband! What a shock he had got that first and happily only wet night, as it turned out!! *Although there was yet to be one other...*

The wedding cards and congratulatory telegrams read like a 'who's who' of Hyson Green! Clac and Sheila Barks, Clac's brother Ned, Sheila's twin sister Pauline, Lenny Waplington and his wife Cynthia, Dereck Smith, Roy Davis a.k.a Roy Minton, Heather and Cyril Potts, Doris and Jeff, Dot and Donny, Freda and Bill. These menfolk were the very backbone of and made the 'Green' what it was in the forties and fifties and still is today to some extent – a colourful and safe place to live.

To a man they all had one thing in common, Hyson Green Boys Club on Archer Street. Here they met and mingled as young impressionable kids under the influence of the club 'skip' Captain A N Gibbs, a stalwart of a man who influenced their thinking and gave them a purpose in life thus turning them into hard working stable young lads with a lot to offer the world. To know them was to love them and where you found one, you would find them all.

I was quickly and reliably informed by the 'lads wives' that no new bride would put a stop to their friendship not that I had ever wanted to I hasten to add, they were great lads and I admired them all and felt privileged to be part of them. Being in their comical company was like being in the middle of a hysterically funny Only Fools and Horse's TV episode. In fact our social life was woven round 'the lads'. Saturday night was 'bring the wives' and we all turned out together, Friday night and Sunday lunch was lads only, as was the aforementioned annual trip to Blackpool.

I think it was Doris that upset the status quo one year by suggesting, almost as a joke, that we turn the tables on the lads and go away to Blackpool ourselves for the weekend to see what the attraction was. It really had been put forward merely in jest at the time, but the idea grew in momentum and became a favourite subject of Saturday night discussion. Not all the wives were in favour of the idea and certainly most of the husbands who would be called upon to swap roles and take on the daunting task of looking after the kids for the weekend and so tried to veto it. Surprisingly mine didn't and was in favour of the idea.

Doris took the money for the trip from us on a weekly basis and we looked forward to it with great glee. It would be the furthest I had ever travelled in my life and so I was doubly excited. Giggling like a bunch of school girls let off the leash, we'd piled onto the bus and the journey had seemed so long. Midway we had stopped off for the ritualistic 'pee and pint' the lads had told us was a must. I don't know who was in the chair so to speak but I found a pint of foaming ale plonked down in front of me. I do not drink. But not wanting to rock the boat I raised my glass and said

19

'cheers' along with the others. I took a sip and dithered, wondering not for the first time, how anyone could drink this muck, get drunk on it and then, as they nursed a banging head on the morrow, say they'd had a good night out! To this day I do not understand it! But I dutifully sipped at the vile beer whilst the girls knocked a few shorts back and in doing so joined their husband's merry school of thought.

At closing time we piled back on the bus and the ladies were just about ready for their beds. I was horrified. You mean we had come all this way and were not going out to paint the town red? I would not let them merely tip into bed I told them, we were going to do as we thought the lads did every year. We arrived at the Apsley hotel in the early hours and the landlady shushed us and told to keep the noise down as the other guests were asleep. We were shown into a room with a double bed and two singles which were instantly commandeered by the other two women. Doris jumped in the double bed with me and I have to confess, the few mouthfuls I had taken of the awful beer had the desired effect, after all my gobbing off, I was the first to fall asleep and in seconds.

Now, you remember me telling you there would be one more time when I would wet the bed...... I awoke in damp horror as Doris got out of bed to clean her teeth. I stayed put and she asked wasn't I coming down for breakfast as the other two had already gone down. I waited until she had gone, washed dressed, raced downstairs and caught the landlady. Shamefaced, I explained what I had done and she said she'd see to it when she cleaned the rooms.

"But I don't want my friend to know."

She was an angel and attended to it whilst we were at breakfast and to this day I was sure Doris never knew. Except....looking for photos to put in the book, I came across a snap of us all out on the town that first night. Doris is on the top row centre wearing a light coloured dress and is aiming a rather smug look in my direction... (I'm third from the left.) Do you suppose...? Hmmmmm....even if she didn't know before, she'll know now!

We spent the first week of our married life off work taking had day and evening trips out, once even getting as far as Nottingham Market Square where we celebrated with a roast beef salad tea in a café there, but mostly to the Lumley Castle pub on the Green or the Carlton on Noel Street where we met up with 'the lads' before going back to bed! (Oh come on, give us a break ...I was only making up for lost time. In our young day there was nowhere to do 'it' was there?)

Our new home opposite the Boulevard pub was a 1st floor 'flat' at the bottom of Hartley Road above a TV shop. It was little more than a cramped bed sitting room really with a separate tiny kitchen, but the landlord thought it qualified for a higher rent if it was called a flat! It was less than a hundred yards away as the crow flies (or is that coughs?) was well within distasteful sniffing distance of the John Players cigarette factory! It didn't do to open the windows and let in fresh air! Raw tobacco is an evil smell. Ugh!

All too soon our supposed 'honeymoon' period was over and the word bride disappeared from my mind as we went back to work. On Monday April the 11th he was up and gone by 7am and didn't reappear until after seven each night. He still went home to his mum every day for a home cooked lunch whilst I grabbed whatever I could. Within that first week, I was up to my neck in housekeeping and after a hard day on a sewing machine at the factory on Peveril Street I dashed home to get dinner on for my beloved. Only now does it occur to me to realise I had found out the hard way that in comparison, marriage to escape a dreaded home life was nowhere near the bed of roses I had romantically envisaged it to be and the roses round our door were simply pigeons on a soot and shit coated window sill! But I have never been afraid of hard work and took it all in my youthful stride.

The Blacknell clan were/are a really nice bunch of folk who welcomed me into their hearts and homes. Father-in-law George was a short wiry strong man with a stubborn nature his daughters-in-law wished he had not passed onto his sons, yet for all that, I loved him. Legend had it he had once played professional football for one of the top north east clubs as a young man but my kids researched it and found nothing. I only ever knew him as a miner. May, my mother in law, was a stout homely kind hearted woman who was very well liked and respected and justifiably so. May was fond of telling the story of her best friend a lady named Pearl who had a son Alan about the same age as John. They were highly intelligent lads who devoured books by the dozen. Pearl and May used to swap 'read' books over to each other. It was only in later years John was to wish he had kept his swaps since Pearl and Alan's surname was Sillitoe! May worked hard in a local pickle factory and you just had to love the scent of pickled onions since she always had a vague whiff of them about her piccalilli stained pinny!

My husband had a handsome and noticeably taller younger blond haired brother David who was married to Brenda, a refined and dainty Newcastle girl, daughter of a banker.

When they had been courting awhile, they got engaged and, her parents invited his parents up to Jesmond in Newcastle for a celebration family dinner. At the dinner table, her father made a speech welcoming David into the family and said how lucky he was to have landed his daughter, such a bonny girl. My mother-in-law May laughingly interrupted his speech and said she was not bonny, she had not a bonny ounce on her and the room was stunned to silence. Fortunately David caught on pretty quickly and roared with laughter to the astonishment of the gathering. He explained that while bonny meant pretty up here in Newcastle, in Nottingham bonny was a kind word for fat!

They married soon after and moved down to Nottingham to live with May and George for a couple of years during which she gave birth to two blond boisterous sons within a very short space of time, namely Paul and Neil. David's job required him to move back north and they did very well for themselves, he eventually becoming a teacher and the last I heard he either managed or owned an English school in Kenya I believe.

The family was completed with an elder sister Iris who lived with her husband Roy and their two daughters Corinne and Jill. He ran his own haulage business from a delightful smallholding in Barrington, a sweet little village on the outskirts of Cambridge with the river Cam running peacefully through it. Their land was a wonderful mish mash of chaos, beauty, noise and charm, interspersed with dozens of animals; from a flock of aggressive geese to dozens of chickens and hens that ran willy nilly everywhere...oh and a three legged dog. The dog had been sleeping peacefully in the long grass when the blades of the mower struck him. Finally, the oldest member of this family was 'Grommar' (grandma) May's mam who was an old lady in her late 80's and had been married at one time to someone connected with Hopewell's the famous Nottingham furniture store. There was a strange aura of racy mystique about her by virtue of historically being the only member of this clan that had *ever* been divorced.

Credit where credit is due though, my husband was a grafter and worked long hours. He started as he meant to go on and at the end of our first week together, he did as his father and grandfather had done before him and dutifully laid my housekeeping on the table. It was £6. The weekly rent alone was £3.50! His mam got the same amount from his dad and she managed very well on it I was told. This was my first but by no means last experience of male chauvinism.

Coming as he did from a long line of 'a man's gotta do what a man's gotta do' Victorian thinkers, my new husband would allow no woman knowledge of what he earned, what bank he had, much less what savings he had or was surely inevitably to amass during our entire married years, whilst being privy to every last penny I earned and having a good 'head of the house' say in what I did with it, mainly maintain the two of us. When I left home at 17, got control of my own wage packet and learned to manage my own money, the first thing I'd done was to open a bank account. So from that very first day I'd always had money behind me even if it had only been a few pounds, it had always been my safety net but that now went by the board.

The household budget I soon found out was totally my responsibility and I was expected to and did cover all the bills; gas, coal, electricity, food and insurances. He was also a stickler for having his made to measure suits expensively cleaned weekly and this was not only another bill for me to foot but I had to take and fetch them back too and he even landed me with his ten shillings a week tailors bill for his new bespoke wedding suit!

By the time I had finished paying out there was precious little or more often than not nothing left of my own wages. Since I'd spent my lifetime being subservient to my mother, it was a habit I didn't think, realise or even know how to break and where today I would have sat my partner down – no on second thoughts; today I would have grabbed him by the scruff of the neck and had a serious nose to nose confrontation about joint finances - back then and for far too many years after, I was too gauche and tipped up my wage packets, indeed simply threw my all into my marriage determined to make it work.

From my digs days in Birmingham, I had learned the art of managing money exceedingly well and this practice had stood me in good stead then and it's a habit I have retained all my life. I took on another job for a couple of pounds a week and became the resident singer at the Wembley club in Sneinton where I also gradually learned the art of being a compere and believe me, it is an art. It was daunting at first but I picked it up and became quite proficient at it. I worked there for about six months and yet for the life of me, I would not even know where to find that club now but for two and odd times, three nights a week back then I sang my heart out and loved it and thankfully the customers loved my singing if not me.

Let me say here and now; I have a lovely singing voice, I cannot take credit for it, it came with the package that included - according to mam - ankles like tree trunks on legs that were bowed big enough to let a pig through to boot, a huge fat arse, a Roman nose that 'roamed all over my face,' (never let it be said mam could find anything beauteous in me!) and a lousy head of hair that needs further comment. Mam would 'rawk' my head raw with a fine toothed comb in an effort to remove 'lugs' that mysteriously appeared in my dull tresses overnight after having been regularly shampooed in green washing soap and barely if at all, rinsed. I had fine brown baby hair that mam said would thicken out as I grew older. Erm, I am nearly 70! Any day now do you think?

In order to assist my lousy head of hair, mam told me I had to eat all my crusts as this helped hair grow, thicken and curl. The woman lies like a cheap carpet! Now let's dwell on the sort of crusts we are talking about here. Not to be confused with mam's idea of crusts, we kids had the stale ones off 'several days old' bread; the green bits of which had been picked off, compared to the wonderful crisp golden brown outer parts of a 'fresh from the baker's oven' loaf mam would enjoy. She would tear them off and eat them lathered in inch thick best butter overlaid with chunks of strong fresh creamy cheese that left behind a clear impression of her teeth.

(I used to think that if she had the 'best'' butter, was the vile tasting aforementioned yellow axle grease that passed for war time 'butter' we kids were forced to eat, as our parents scoffed our share of the rationed stuff, the 'worst' butter?)

The soft middle of the remainder of the loaf was divvied up between us kids. It only occurs to me now to wonder why mam also had a lousy head of hair and yet look at how many crusts she devoured! And Sandra was damn near bald until she was about five and yet today has the best head of hair of all of us.

But following mam's 'tongue in cheek' advice, I ate not only my crusts but also everybody else's too totally unaware that in doing so, I was adding to the chunk of my legs and the fat of my backside! This habit has stayed with me all my life and the first and last slices of bread, crusts of course, are always the first to go. I LOVE 'em and while my hair has stayed resolutely thin, straight and refuses to grow, my backside, legs and ankles have got thicker by the crust! So I do admire good heads of hair and many's the woman I would have swapped half my oversized bosom with, having only ever once found someone with a worse head of hair than mine and hers was the colour and texture of an old factory yard brush.

(And talking of bosoms; I have always been well blessed in that department. One boyfriend told his pal at work that I had the most magnificent breasts he had ever seen (I may have afforded him the privilege of touching, but he hadn't 'seen' them actually!) and that they must have been at least 38inches and yet I was good to look at in the face too! His pal replied "I wouldn't give a damn if she didn't have a face at all as long as she had big breasts! LOL!)

Come on girls. Trip down memory lane with me on this one: In those days, women didn't have their hair 'done' they had it set! In the 1960's along with the majority of fashionable females, I adopted the 'Beehive' hairdo. This was a complicated arrangement of back combed or French frizzed hair which was teased into large barrel-like rolls, pinned up with dozens of steel hair pins, gripped high on the

27

crown of the head and heavily sprayed into place with hair lacquer as strong as yacht varnish. Getting it 'set' - and believe me, the lacquer did just that - was one thing, keeping it that way, quite another. Short of sleeping upright, or with one's head in a box, it was a real problem. Conventional hair nets did not do the job but someone had the bright idea of pulling a pair of elastic knickers carefully over her head in a bid to keep it tidy. This 'hairnet' idea was achieved by stretching the pants over the elbow of one arm and with the other stretching them wide and very carefully putting one's head inside and securing it in place over the barrel curls. It worked and the idea caught on. Henceforth we ladies wore two pairs of pants to bed! The next morning we carefully lifted them off and after pinning back a few stray hairs, plastered it down again with the aforementioned liquid cement hairspray. Depending on how well the hair was protected by this 'net', this style could and would be made to last many weeks by some cash strapped ladies and you can include me amongst them.

After a few weeks of this, probably the first of the now well known urban legends was born. The story that was passed mouth to aghast mouth and probably single handedly killed off this style, was that someone knew of a woman who knew of another woman's next door neighbour's relative who'd had her hair set and followed the routine as described above. After a few weeks, her head began to itch (and oh, didn't it girls?) Then she felt a bit of pain which got worse to the point where she went to her doctors and it was discovered that a large insect known colloquially as a blackclock (I think its correct term is rain beetle) had made a nest and laid her eggs in the thatch and her young had begun to eat their way into her brain! Another legend was that a

28

*stray hairpin had found its way into the brain of someone who knew someone who knew...oh you get the idea, and paralysed her! Of course it goes without saying **I** didn't believe it. It just so happened I chose another hair style. I **did** I tell you!*

CHAPTER 2.

LAURA.

I had been wed only a matter of a few weeks or so when something really odd happened. Let me say here and now, I do not believe in ghosties, beasties or things that go bump in the night but even so..... I clearly recall it was a Sunday afternoon and that mournful programme 'Sing Something Simple' - or as I had re-named it 'Music to commit suicide to', such was its dirge like content - was playing softly on the radio. I was weepy and restless, walking from one room to the other and back again. It was not at all like me and John asked me what was wrong. I said I didn't know but something was. I got more and more distressed. Then there was an unusual knock at the door. Visitors we didn't have, my husband I had found out was almost anti social and would totally ignore anyone who came to the flat and, even in later homes we had together, would pick up a newspaper and hide behind it much to my chagrin. It was the landlord and he asked for me. He told me my youngest brother Dereck aged 7 was desperately ill and I needed to go home at once. I raced on foot the mile or so and got there just as they were closing the ambulance door. I jumped in with mam.

He was taken at great speed and with alarm bells clanging to the City Hospital and there he was diagnosed with several ailments amongst which were measles, mumps, meningitis and **malnutrition.** And let this be a lesson to all who refuse to eat properly as he did. Essential vitamins were missing in his diet and it very nearly killed him. You could say many things about mam but she did feed us a balanced diet of good albeit simple food as far as her purse would permit. Junk food was *not* an option. But as we all know, you can take a horse to water....

In those days, if you were dangerously ill the Nottingham health department used to place a small ad in the Post that gave a number relating to a patient and Derecks was F150. It only occurs to me now to wonder why the need to publish this. Derecks number was in the paper for weeks. We were not allowed to come into contact with him and could only speak to him through a window. He looked wan thin and fragile and it really was touch and go for many weeks. Then, one day, mam and I went together to see him and he wept bitterly for the first time and pleaded to be allowed to come home. We left in floods of tears and mam was convinced he would die that day. The following day they said he could come home and he did. I can assure you *this* horse **was** led to water and forced to drink but fast after that!

Within a matter of a few days of him coming home, I found out I was pregnant. To say it was a shock is putting it mildly and I blamed it on my brother's illness. Reeling as I undoubtedly did from the news, I also took in the miracle that was happening within me but at the same time began to worry how I would manage with a baby as well as a full time job. My beloved was absolutely no help; his mum had worked all her married life and he told me he expected me to do the same. That his mum lived with HER mum and so had a lifelong on site mother's help, baby sitter, cook/ housekeeper, laundress, cleaner and bottle washer didn't occur to him. But with the resilience of youth, I adapted pretty quickly and by the end of that first week, I had bought my expected 'son' Joseph John a pair of blue pods (baby shoes) and week on week added to my layette until I had enough blue baby clothes and boy like toys for triplets.

We now had to move of course. With a baby on the way, we would need more room and I found a flat almost next door to The Grande pub at the bottom of the hill on Alfreton Road and was no more than a few hundred yards away from our parents and in-law's houses. It was a pound dearer at £4.50p a week. It may not sound much of an increase but it was *huge*. My parents three storey terraced house with three bedrooms cost even less than a quarter of this but there were no houses of any kind to rent anywhere – and trust me, I distastefully but desperately chased after many a one wherein someone had died only hours earlier. In those days married couples mainly lived with in-laws, something neither of us wanted or could have tolerated.

Our flat was a nice big place admittedly and we had the whole ground floor consisting of a large living room, kitchen, a nice big bedroom and a shared first floor bathroom but since this was blocked by a baby gate, we continued to use our kitchen to wash and the public baths to bathe. Upstairs lived another family whom I never got to know beyond hearing them calling to a baby daughter named Lulu. I bloomed; my skin and hair never looked so good. Six months into the pregnancy I was told by work that I had to take maternity leave from the following week, though I was loathe leaving the financial comfort of my wages. Even so, I remember that first week's freedom from the noisy screaming machines of work as being pure bliss.

The weather was wonderfully warm as I recall and though I had a bump it was barely noticeable and I was still working at the Wembley Club. I was in fine spirits that Friday morning and was singing my head off as I got ready to go and fetch my last week's wages. Suddenly and with no warning, all hell broke loose. Totally alone in the house, my waters broke. There seemed to be gallons of it and I staggered around not knowing what to do. Frantically donning my coat I hurriedly made for the doctors surgery, this being about half a mile away. I explained what had happened to the receptionist and she got me in to see the doctor immediately. After a brief examination, he was sure the baby's head was pressing on my bladder, I was instinctively sure he was wrong.

He bid me go home and go to bed and he would come see me as soon as surgery had finished. But I was just around the corner from Beal's and called in to get my much needed last wage packet. I then shopped en route home and got something for John's tea and when I got back it was to discover the doctor waiting for me on the doorstep. He was not best pleased that I hadn't followed his instructions. He bid me jump in his car and took me off to the hospital himself. Do bear in mind, there were little or no telephones and so no way of letting anyone know where I was or what had happened.

He took me to the City hospital and straight to the required maternity department, gave me a sealed letter to give to the staff and said he would call and see me later. As I went into the room it was full of ladies in various stages of pregnancy and the nurse took my letter, gave me a ticket numbered 101 and bid me sit down. The chairs were in rows like a classroom and I sat at the back. A disembodied voice over the Tannoy called number 12 into the examination room! I could see I was going to be here for hours.

I had only been sat for about 2 minutes and already my coat was saturated. I grabbed a passing nurse's arm and asked could she find me a towel. She smiled reassuringly and went off to get one. She had walked maybe three or four steps, stopped, turned on her heel, came back and with a puzzled expression on her face asked why I needed one? I innocently replied my waters had broken. In a panic she asked why I had not told her. I replied that I had given her the note from the doctors and as far as I was aware, all these women could have been in the same state. I was a novice to all this.

Wow, did they ever move fast. Within minutes I was in a wheelchair being raced along busy hospital corridors and was put on a bed in a small delivery room. A nurse came in and undressed me, putting me in a white cotton tie down the front bed gown. I was panic stricken, deathly afraid and horribly lonely. Nobody even knew where I was. I learned later that a policeman was despatched to John's workplace in Radford and he was told. Delivery rooms are frightening places for anyone, even experienced mums, let alone a novice like me and I was no exception to this being overwhelmed by the strange sounds, smells and what looked to be tortuous stainless steel instruments lying elbow close on a trolley alongside my bed, neatly lined up in readiness, but in readiness for *what*?

All around me women in their own cubicles were shouting, crying and sometimes screaming out in pain as anonymous muffled voices urged them to 'push' or conflictingly, 'don't push', somehow I didn't think they were having lessons on how to cross the road with a pram! For the first time it occurred to me the screaming orchestra was a sign that giving birth to this baby was going to be painful. About every 20 minutes or so, the door opened and a masked face appeared and asked was I ok. I'd say yes and the face would disappear. After about an hour a young female doctor came in.

Fear welled up in my throat again. I will never ever forget this woman the longest day I live and breathe. Her name was Dr Stringer and it suited her since she had long black frizzy and string like hair. My sense of fear rose off the graph as she stretched out her hand to reach for one of those hideous instruments off the table but to my relief she merely picked up a pair of rubber gloves and after donning them, examined me, told me I was in labour and asked was the pain strong? I rightly told her I had no pain. She placed her hands on my stomach and told me I was having contractions.

"There! Did you feel that?"

I stared blankly and painlessly back at her and shook my head.

"There's no need to be brave, you must have felt that pain?"

"No, I am not trying to be brave; there is no pain, honestly".

She then sent me spiralling into further fear and despair as she uttered these forever remembered cruel words;

"Well whether you can or not, you are going to lose this baby."

I immediately howled. Accident this baby may well have been but I had got used to him sharing my body and had talked to him daily about life and what we would do together and even sang lullabies to him. I didn't want to lose my son. She slapped my leg and as she turned to leave, told me over her shoulder, I was very young and had all the time in the world to have dozens of babies. The door closed behind her and I was left in floods of tears.

I lay there alone and distraught for a couple of hours with only the occasional head poked round the door to ask if I was ok, until the frantically busy staff finally realised I really wasn't in labour and then they moved me and my bed onto Livingstone ward. I was put into a bed-space over which was a large sign that said I was in the care of a local hero of a man by the name of Dr Cochrane. His name meant nothing to me but everyone talked of him in reverent tones. As soon as I was left alone, I got dressed back into my own clothes convinced now they would send me home.

At some time that day the God like revered doctor Cochrane appeared at my bedside. He was a strong thick set man with very hairy arms and spoke in a clipped no nonsense Scottish accent. He felt my tummy with surprisingly gentle hands as in keen concentration he looked over my head into the distance.

"Ye'll have ter stay in hospital until this baby's born. I want you to stay in bed, don't get out, not even to go to the toilet, use the bed pan." He said firmly, his words reverberating around my disbelieving head. I had honestly expected to be sent home the minute it was found out that I was not in labour. Just a few days away, I was to turn 21 and was desperate to go home to celebrate the day.

"But..." despite myself I began to well up, "will I be home by Thursday? It's my 21st birthday." I explained tearfully through the huge lump in my throat.

"Och no lassie, you'll be here a fair few months." I wailed and he said;

"Don't take on so; I'll get the kitchen to bake ye a birthday cake with 21 candles."

He patted my hand, left me and I once more dissolved into tears. Tutting, the nurse undressed me and put me back in the white shroud of a hospital bed gown.

My pounding scared heart gradually settled down somewhat and at 7 that night my husband came to see me. He looked every bit as scared as I felt. He came bearing a newly bought 'sensible' nightie and gifts from his mum of cakes she had proudly made without benefit of a set of scales! Bless, I loved May to bits and whilst she was an excellent cook, she could not bake to save her life. My sister-in-law Brenda had known I didn't possess a dressing gown and had loaned me a pretty pink one of hers. I could not settle into the routine of the hospital and each day I awoke what little sleep I'd had willing the staff to send me home, loath to believe it wasn't going to happen.

Now, do bear in mind I was an entrenched smoker and had been for a good few years by now. Not permitted to get out of bed, I had to grab a smoke as and when I could. Each time I needed to use the hated bedpan, I used the screen as a way of getting a quick drag and one never to be forgotten day under cover of the screen, I stretched out to get my fags out of the bedside cabinet, or should I say I *over*-stretched and fell with an almighty thump! It was a fall that was to prove costly to me. I scrambled back up quickly but the nurse had seen or heard my fall and came rushing. I was told off and my fags were confiscated.

That night I was able to get more fags off my husband and managed to have a much needed swift drag under the blankets! He left at 8pm and I waved him goodbye. I watched as he left and as the door slowly closed behind him, the most almighty pain I had ever experienced in my entire life shot through me and sent me writhing to the bottom of the bed in a loud agony I generously shared with the whole of the ward not to say entire block!! So this is what all the screaming had been about. I felt as if I had been hit by a bus. My due date had been given as Nov 20th. It was the 12th of

September 1960. Alerted by my neighbour, the nurse came and examined my bump.

"You are not having contractions. You have a few months to go yet," she said, pulling my bedclothes back and walking away. A couple of days ago, for several hours I had been told I was in labour and I had protested I wasn't and now that I was, the nurse didn't believe me. It was shaping up to be a long painful night.

At about eleven, my continued battle with this awesome pain had kept the ward awake and eventually the nurse on duty sent for a trolley to take me to the delivery room. Such was my agony I could not even get onto the trolley without help. I was about to find out that night that not all nurses are Florence Nightingales! *(This was reinforced for me when I recently trod on a darning needle and had it snap off in my foot and ended up in the Queens Medical Hosp overnight and fell foul of the staff nurse!)*

The non F N nurse helped me climb on the trolley and then said; 'I will see you in the morning you mardy cow, perhaps now my patients can get some sleep.' I instantly screeched at her; 'If I could get off this trolley I would bloody bash you one.' And I would have too. Some people should not be nurses.

I was taken in a lift to the delivery room frantically trying to hang onto the sides of the trolley as I thrashed about in almost continued agony and once there was instantly surrounded by caring doctors and nurses. There then followed a long almost three hour battle of pain, exhaustion and more searing pain. This son of mine had no idea of his due date and was on his way right NOW. But he had hit a problem; he was stuck fast and no amount of tugging whilst I screamed made any difference.

I was told to hang on tightly to the bed edge as they were going to have to cut him out. Those of you of a queasy disposition who know no better, have my permission to believe it was my tummy they cut but as I was in so much agony anyway, I didn't feel it. Then at 2.05 am he was born only 'he' was a 'she' and she was a tiny scrap of a thing all bone and slack skin blackened by pressure. The doctor passed her over the bed to the nurse and they guestimated her weight as being between 2 and 3 lb. The nurse weighed her. "I win! 2lb 3oz," she said and bought her to my side to see.

She was incredibly tiny with high sharp cheek bones and her shiny wet hair the colour of jet, was a mass of tiny plastered to the head curls and waves. Her 'father inherited' deep furrowed frown marks on her brow let us all know she was not best pleased. I stared transfixed at her.

"She is the image of her father," I sobbed.

"Oh such fanciful talk from you mothers, you are all the same," the nurse said, wrapping the baby up tightly in a towel.

"Is she going to be alright?" I asked the doctor my bottom lip going.

"She is one of the tiniest we have ever had. Don't expect too much, it will be a miracle if she makes it to the morning." Refusing to sugar coat his words his voice was sympathetic but firm. Now there was a race on to get her to an incubator and in the last split second as I gazed at her, time stood still. She looked like a skinned rabbit and was without doubt the ugliest baby I had ever seen, she was also without the slightest shadow of a doubt the most beautiful baby I had ever seen.

"You will need to name her; she has to be christened immediately." The nurse explained.

"Amanda May" I said automatically.

Her black almost marble sized eyes stared blindly back at me before she was raced away to an incubator and my last sight was of her fingers spread wide, and as the nurse hurriedly took her out of the room, I never took my eyes off her.. And if you think I can relate this without recourse to floods of tears.....

Now it seems *I* was in trouble. For reasons unknown to me, my afterbirth was held fast and I was put through the mill in their efforts to release it. It was a race against the clock and through a red mist of the most agonistic pain, they did their best to free it. But their efforts proved useless and they finally agreed I had to be operated on. It being by now about 3am, time was of the essence and there was certainly no time to get a permission signature from my husband for the op and so I had to sign it for myself. I would love to see that signature today. I was then injected and instantly was freed from that awe inspiring pain as the injection took immediate effect.

I awoke at dawn and was lying in a side ward, covered with blankets and free of pain. It is legendary that childbirth labour is the hardest pain to bear and the quickest to forget and I hereby testify to that. Memories of the previous day came flooding back and as I quietly lay there, it quickly dawned on me I was now a mother. My stomach freed from a moving baby felt strangely still and quiet. Over the bed head hanging on the wall were a pair of earphones and the radio was playing softly through them. Frank Sinatra was singing Laura. As the beautiful refrains washed over me, I decided I would re-name her Laura and, because of the time of day, I would give her the middle name of Dawn. When I later told the nurse of the name change she told me she had just spent an hour making out all the documentation and refused to change it. To this day her record at the City Hospital Nottingham is in the name of Amanda May! I spent my 21st birthday in hospital and John bought me a pile of cards and gifts from family and friends. As I opened them the nurse who helped delivers my baby passed by. She stopped and asked was this my husband. I said yes and she said "I take it back, that baby is the very spit of him." And so she was. My kids know who their father is and many's the time I have told them that if in later years they have a DNA test done and it comes back that he is NOT their father, then I am not their mother.

I came home a few days later and was put to bed for 10 days and left alone in the flat, there being no such sensible thing as maternity leave for fathers then despite at that time, my desperate need. The midwife came in a couple of times a day, mam and also odd friends visited but the rest of the time I was alone for hours on end and worried sick about the baby. Oh for a phone... Each day someone got news to me. First she lost weight and went down below 2lb then there was elation as she put back on a quarter of an ounce!!! After three days I could stand it no longer. Waiting until after the midwife had done her daily duty by me, I got out of bed, took two buses to the hospital and went to see her for myself.

I was not allowed into the premature baby unit and had to stand outside as a somewhat surprised nurse bought the cot to the window for me to see her. There were several cots which were homes to wan limp sickly little souls but my baby was the opposite. Her legs and feet were moving furiously and her hands, still with the fingers spread wide, were punching the air. She looked angry and cross as though blaming

41

someone, anyone, for her predicament. She was so...vigorous.

After a mere couple of minutes, the nurse returned her cot whence it had come and came out to me. She questioned what I was doing here after so short a time of bed-rest and I told her how worried I had been. She kindly told me not to make the journey again pointing out the baby would need me to be well and strong for when she came out of hospital. I returned home absolutely drained but I carried the picture in my mind of my warrior daughter and I was at peace. I kind of knew she would be ok now.

That evening the midwife called in and at the same time mam turned up too. Horrified she told mam the hospital had phoned her and told her where I had been and the two women bundled up all my shoes and mam took them away thus ensuring I remained bed bound and again, alone for hours on end. With only a portable radio for company and rumbling traffic just a few yards away from where I languished in my bed, I obediently set my mind to rest for the requisite number of days. Well, that was the supposed plan anyway.....

CHAPTER 3

DURBAN TERRACE

About now, a friend of a friends next door neighbours aunties uncle, (oh you know who I mean, he used to chew bread for the slab square pigeons and was the founder of the now well known urban legends!) passed on the information that a few derelict old houses were being temporarily un-condemned, opened up and deemed fit for use once more after being closed up as unfit for donkeys years by the Nottingham City Council, a council desperate to relieve the acute shortage of accommodation in those days. My mother returned my shoes to me pronto and exhorted me to get out of bed and go after one like NOW and I did, racing there well ahead of the field. There was a limited life expectancy of this part of the Green and the house was scheduled for eventual demolition, the promise being that when that happened we'd be given a council house.

I went to see the landlord, took with me several references from, amongst others, our two previous landlords and also our respective bosses and pleaded ours and our new baby's case. He examined the references carefully studied me over the top of his wire framed glasses for a moment and reached behind him to a board full of keys. He selected a set and asked me if I wanted to view this one? It would be £3.00 a week plus a one off payment of £5 key money. I blenched at the key money but it had to be found. (Key money was a 'bunce' for someone but I am not sure in this instance who received it.) But even with the key money to pay, it was still a whole £1.50 a week cheaper than our present flat. The small white paper key fob read 12 Durban Terrace, Hyson Green. I sped on winged feet and raced up the steep hill to what was to be our first real home.

Here there was a few more scents to get acclimatised to; as well as the sooty stink from the hundreds of puthering chimneys; the strong yeasty smell of the Shipstone's Brewery just a stones throw away mingled with the heavy washing powder odours from the public wash house a few feet above the terrace chimney pots and if the wind was in the right direction, the soap factory would occasionally smother us briefly in the most beautiful perfumes. This seemingly neat little terrace with 7 houses either side of a wide quarry tiled paved area was accessed off Fisher Street through a low walled gateway opening, the gate of which had long since gone had there ever been one. Its very neatness belied what I was about to find.

Ours was the farthest one on the left. The end of the terrace was walled and backed onto the wash-house/baths on Noel Street and our roof was level with its yard and so the house would prove to be really dark, the light having to be left on day and night. I put the key in the lock and expectantly pushed it but though the lock sprang, it would not budge. I peered through umpteen years of accumulated dirt on the windows and saw it was crammed wall to wall and almost to the ceiling with various amounts of rubble and tons of thick leather off cuts. I was to find that no amount of subsequent cleaning made a deal of difference to those windows. I went round the rear and unlocked the back door. Access was not much easier. The house was minute, consisting of just four rooms and was jaw droppingly old, neglected and bad.

My nose was instantly assaulted with an odd mixture of damp stale air, musty and fusty with an under scent of old leather. The kitchen was I judged, no more than approximately six foot square and this led to a front room some ten foot by eight. But again, I could barely get past the years of rubble piled high to the door. The staircase was off the kitchen on my immediate right but the last three steps were missing as was floor under the sink and there were huge yawning black holes exposing the coal cellar below and that in turn had its own scent reminiscent of the Moffat Street cellar.

By treading on a piece of wood still clinging to the side of the stair tread, I managed to breach the yawning gap, reach the hand rail and hauled myself up the rest of the stairs where I found two tiny bedrooms. Thankfully there was no stored junk up there only a few million webs occupied by optimistic but exceedingly misguided and thin spiders. Out back was an unevenly brick paved long communal shared yard with a row of disgusting toilets the roofs of which were falling in and smack in the middle of them was a wide opening to a noisy leather factory the scent of which was overpowering and its mighty machinery hummed with activity day and night.

As well as the problem of the stairs and the missing floorboards in the kitchen, there was neither electricity nor gas and I was later to find out, the living room floor bounced when walked on. The vibrations caused by merely walking across the room eased the drawers out of the baby's clothes chest and unless I pushed them back every few minutes, the whole lot would topple over and there was no such thing as sue the landlord in those days! We were told we would have to put the house right ourselves if we wanted it. We'd got a choice?

The two downstairs rooms had obviously been used to store all this unwanted rubbish belonging to the factory in the back yard and they didn't want to know. As my hubby was at work all day, it fell to me to clear it and on top of the fatigue of the child bearing ordeal I had just been through, it was really hard work but as bad as the house was, I thought myself privileged to have a roof over my family's heads. We women take on anything. Like the proverbial mother hen, I ruffled my feathers and began to make my nest. As the room slowly began to empty I became aware that the previous owners of many years ago had left behind some furniture and it was quality stuff too. There were two 1920's stylish red real leather armchairs (wish I still that them!) and a small sideboard with a cocktail cabinet in it and when you have nothing...

(When we finally left that house my in-laws Brenda and David came down with a van and took those chairs back to Newcastle with them!)

In the kitchen there was an old black three burner iron stove not nearly as elegant as and far older than the Moffat Street one my mother had cooked so well on. Friends rallied round and helped us. One made the floor good, one the stairs, we paid for the gas and electricity to be connected up ourselves - I seem to remember it costing a massive £15 and once they were working I set to, to make us our first real home, often still working on it until the early hours. It just had to be ready in time for the baby to come out of hospital. (In all the years we were wed, I was never able to make my husband see the wisdom of owning one's own home and the money we spent on that dump would I am sure in those days have paid the deposit on a new one. The phrase 'chucking good money after bad' comes readily to mind.)

Next door but one lived an old school friend of my husband and he very kindly wallpapered our sitting room free of charge. Folk did things like that for each other back then. When I went back the next day I was surprised that the wallpaper either side of the fireplace was still very wet and so it was the day after and the day after and even unto the day we finally left three years later. It took a while to dawn on me that the baths and wash house above us had oceans of water draining away every hour and much of it drained right down our internal wall.

We were to find out we had some colourful neighbours. One lady who lived across the terrace from me was wed to a man who was allergic...to work! It wasn't that he couldn't *keep* a job; he would not *have* a job in the first place no matter how good or well paid it was. It interfered with his hobby which was drinking. In those days and I don't know that it has been repealed, there was a law that said a man HAD to keep his wife and children, failure to do so would result in a court appearance and a gaol sentence of a few weeks. After a few years the powers that be gave up on him and he was allowed to claim for his wife and children and lived soley on benefits. He so liked his 'pop' as he called it, that he rarely made it home with his dole money intact. So drunken rows were a regular occurrence and often he locked his naked wife out of their house and her door hammering and shouting would go on until the early hours.

One afternoon he came home the worse for drink having spent all his dole money and she hit him with a frying pan which she screamed, should have been full of the meat he'd failed to bring home! Ears ringing, he stormed out of the house and the next morning she fetched me across to see what he had done. Late the previous night she had been sat quietly dozing by the fire waiting for him to come home and had been rudely woken by him screaming at her to get the frying pan working and he threw a large object onto the sofa alongside her. It was half a cow and a few tons of sausages!

With moving to and working on the house, I was too busy and too far away to do the Wembley club anymore and I reluctantly gave it up. I did as my mother had done before me and went to the Pownalls rag shop looking for bedding and blankets.

*(Here I again interject to answer comments made by a caller on a phone in programme on BBC radio Nottingham. He said I had got it wrong in my book when I talked of Pownalls rag shop and that Pownalls never owned a rag shop and was in fact a scrap metal merchant. Yes he was a scrap0 metal merchant and yes he **did** own a rag shop and he also had at least one son who had a pitch on the Sneinton market selling fancy ornaments pots and china. He would lift and throw into the air a huge basket of crockery and catch it without cracking as much as a saucer. Trust me the Pownalls had many differing business interests.)*

Like my mother before me, I also became a frequent visitor to the old Central and Sneinton second hand markets on the lookout for things to furnish my home with and that dubious set of single sheets we had been given as a wedding present now came into their own as I died them a deep pink and used them as curtains for Laura's bedroom. With time, patience and pennies not to mention a lot of hard work, I gradually turned that dump into a facsimile of a reasonable home and with one eye on the damp that cascaded down the walls from the above wash house, I even borrowed a small electric fire to air the babies room out and make it more pleasant for her when she finally came home.

It was to be a long battle for Laura to make the necessary 5lb (I believe its 6lb today) before they would allow her to come out which they finally did on Jan 6th the following year. I came home with her in a taxi and the first people I called on were my family. My brothers and sisters were delighted with this tiny little scrap. Mam told me to wait until she got to our house the next morning as she wanted to watch me bathe her. Right! I thought not. The last thing I needed now was to have her dent my confidence by telling me I was doing it all wrong and by the time she arrived at 8am, Laura was bathed, fed and sound asleep, much to mam's chagrin. I knew my mother very well and my belief that she would undermine my confidence was proved right when at my subsequent post natal I was advised by the paediatrician to start giving Laura the yolk of an egg. Mam called me a liar and threatened to complain to the health authority and have the baby taken away from me. It seems she was to make as good a grandma to my kids as she had been a mother to me. Sad.

Having missed out on this Christmas, I was going to make sure she had a good one at the end of 1961! You just see little one.... Even though she had more than doubled her birth weight, she was still incredibly tiny. Most folk were afraid to pick her up but as I had no other child to compare her with, treated her as a normal baby and she thrived. Mam put her expert knitting skills to good use and made her a whole layette of doll sized baby clothes and mother-in-law May bought her something every week. What with those things and the seemingly hundreds of dresses and night gowns I made from remnants bought cheaply off the market, I will say this, hard up or not, no baby had better clothes than mine did, I made damn sure of that.

My thoughtless husband gave me not one penny more to run the house but this tiny baby had to have something called True Food and where the National Dried baby milk from the clinic was about 1/6d a ton, this stuff was a massive 14/- a small box. It was the very best you could possibly buy but if she was to have a chance at life she *HAD* to have it I was told by the hospital and have it she did.

(That True Food was a miracle and in a very short time, I watched my baby's face plump out and she was a little blonde curly haired beauty. I had been warned that she would not catch up with normal birth rate children until she was as old as possibly three or four but within twelve months she had caught up with and was racing past other babies. This kid of mine had a lot of living to do.)

I cut back on everything I could, even the rent and insurances to ensure she came first but when my husband found out I had not paid the rent there was an almighty row and his mum pointedly asked if I could not pay one weeks rent how on earth could I pay two? She was of course quite right. Reluctantly 6 weeks later I found a good reliable local baby sitter and the following week went back out to work full time. Mam was furious with me and lost no time telling me what a lousy mother I was but she had no idea of the problems I had and I was not about to tell her. I thought myself lucky to have found a minder who agreed to take Laura on despite her frailty and not be afraid. I in turn looked after the lady very well financially. That settled I got a job with a fairly small local firm called Adelina's on Northgate. It was just a brisk ten minute walk away and I took it in my stride and quickly got my finances back under control once more.

As with all things, the baby minder was not to last and within a few months; I was once more looking for a solution to my problem. I found one in the form of an old neighbour from my Moffat Street days. This lady would change her nappies and put the unwrapped soiled ones directly under the pram mattress. Within a few days the pram stank rotten. I started to put newspapers under the mattress and asked her to wrap them first but she continued in her own not so sweet way. I talked my predicament over with May and she very kindly offered to have Laura for me when she finished work every afternoon, now all I had to do was persuade mam to help me out in the mornings. She, like May, worked shifts and could have helped me with the baby. But she refused and I had no choice but to take her away from the minder and not wanting to go down that path again, got her into a good nursery close by. It was *much* more expensive but totally efficient, caring and absolutely 100% reliable. I just had to work that bit harder to meet the bill.

Like all parents what we never had as kids, we made sure our offspring did not miss out on in their young day. Sweeties and chocolates were very few and far between when we were kids, partly because they were rationed and needed coupons but mainly because we didn't have the pennies to buy them. There had been some things that were 'off ration' like the huge colour changing gob stoppers, or packets of Kali (sherbet) which was a wonderfully sharp lemon powder eaten almost ritualistically by wetting ones fore finger – the same finger that had half a bottle of black school ink soaked into it from the use of the leaky school pens – and the residue (both of them!) were then deliciously and happily sucked off.

There had also been other non sweet alternatives on which to spend one's halfpennies pocket money worthy of a mention but not necessarily a taste, such as Tiger nuts, hard little misshapen dried things that released into the chewer's mouth a sweet milky taste. Locust sticks which were long rock hard inch wide dried flat beans a little like broad beans and were shiny brown on the outside and a sort of banana yellow with the consistency of 'washing up bowl plastic' on the inside and had seeds like, well, broad beans. They took a long time to devour. One bit into it, tugged hard with good strong teeth undamaged by sweets and sugar and tore off a lump to chew. They are in fact used as cattle feed today and I don't know that they weren't intended as such even then, but they were sweet, coupon free and cheap enough at a halfpenny each for us to eat on an almost daily basis. I can't say I particularly liked them but I did eat a good few....until the day I bit into one and a *half* big fat maggot dropped out!

Then there were liquorice sticks; these were about 3 inches long, rock hard and tasted bitter. On a similar vein were Imps, tiny hard little strong tasting black liquorice bits that were awful but not as awful as those liquorice roots we used to chew. Oh these were dreadful and were bits of dried hard root that yielded some sort of horrid woody sweetness that stained the lips and tongue the brightest yellow. We had many a childhood malaise but with so much liquorice about, constipation was not one of them! As it was I found myself calling in and buying Laura sweets and chocolate on the way home every single night, so guilt ridden was I at having to leave her and to this day she has the sweetest of teeth through which she curses me!

John went out on the booze with his mates every single night, sometimes this would be before he came home from work or he would eat, dress and run. He was not faultless but I can honestly say womanising was not one of the few he had. Occasionally May and George would baby-sit and I would accompany him on a night out with the lads. Sometime in that year we went to a dance at the Commodore. As usual, I got up to sing and was asked if I wanted the job as the resident singer with the Malcolm Allen band. I jumped at the chance and then found out I had been offered this job at least twice before but they had asked my husband and he had refused it. I was not happy and had a rare row with him. He agreed reluctantly, I might add, to baby-sit the odd nights I would sing.

The arrangement worked well and I had a good rapport with the lads; Dougie Parmenter on accordion, Big John Harrison on what else but big base. He was known as Big John on account of being tall enough to pick up the base, tuck it under his chin and play it like a violin (ok, I exaggerate!) He would play it and at times fall asleep on it (and now I don't exaggerate!) - Malcolm Draper played an exquisite piano, Gil Lee was on drums, Alan Meakin on sax and Eric White on trumpet. They were wonderful musicians individually, together they were superb. It only paid £1.50 a four hour night and sometimes for only one night a week, other times 2 or 3 nights and this involved having babysitters in. The lads sometimes did private gigs and I was invited in on them too and we once played the Canadian air base at Langar and what a night that was. We came home with carrier bags full of otherwise unobtainable goodies from the equivalent of their NAAFI.

I remember us doing the Loughborough college 'end of rag week' celebrations. The main attraction was the Kenny Ball jazz band and we were in an adjacent smaller room. The ballroom was fairly empty to begin with and we treated it as a rehearsal night and did our own thing. With no strict ballroom dancing tempo to worry about, we dragged our rhythms and beats to suit ourselves. We did all the old classics like Sunday Kind of Love, Body and Soul and East Of the Sun (and West of the Moon). It was a truly wonderful magic night and gradually Kenny Ball lost his entire audience as one by one, couple by couple drifted in to us and sat in rapt attention on the floor at our feet. A few weeks later, at another gig in Derbyshire somewhere, I met Mike and Bernie Winters and also Jack Hulbert and Cecily Courtney (ask your *great* grandma!) What fun these gigs were. But from these at times, very glamorous occasions, I nightly returned to my beyond humble home with the sound of Eric White's trumpet still screaming in my ears thus making sleep impossible.

Little aside here; don't kid yourself, very few of us are easy to live with and when I finally did get a decent house with the miracle of a bathroom, I was to find the best way for me to relax and get the music out of my head after a gig, was to have a late night bath. Bliss, err, just one thing, I have a stupid aversion to drying myself. To avoid it, I would normally clean the bathroom from end to end and slowly drip dry. But at 2 or 3 am, it was too noisy an occupation so I would light the blue touch paper by getting into bed with my husband sopping wet through! Whhhoooosh!

Life plodded on and as September the 13th came round, I took Laura to Studio Loraine in town and had her birthday portrait taken. A few days later, I had to go back to pick up the proofs and asked my father-in-law George would he mind keeping an eye on her whilst I went into town. He was more than willing having offered many times before. I wheeled her in to their sitting room in her pram and shot off into town. When I got to the studio I was rewarded by seeing a huge blow up shot of my beautiful baby hung smack bang in the middle of the street window! Wow! I raced back not wanting to leave Laura one second longer than I needed to. What a sight greeted me. It was automatic no matter who had sat with her to ask even as I walked through the door, had she been ok. Oh she had been fine said George. I gave her something to play with and she was no trouble. The something he had 'given her to play with' was the Sunday lunch chicken carcase and she had pulled it to bits in the pram. Now come on....you could NOT make this up! I was later to go on and leave my second baby with him on another occasion after warning him not to be so daft this time. When I got back, he had given her a sweet which had naturally stuck her fingers up and then he had given her a feather to play with and she had spent the entire hour patiently pulling it off one hand and onto the other! It was innovative to say the least.

Christmas was almost upon us again and I set out to honour my promise and make it a really important time for my beloved baby. I had bought her many gifts – oh nothing expensive you understand and had decorated our tiny living room for her. I had decided to give a little supper party after pub closing time for a few of our close friends as I had a time or two before and on that Christmas Eve I had put in the oven a huge pot of shin of beef tenderly stewing it all day. I was looking forward to entertaining any or all, of them; Smithy, Lennie Waplington, Jeff and Doris Marshall, Dot and Donnie Sheila and Clac, Freda and Bill and Pam and Nobby. It would be a squeeze to get them all in but hey, it was Christmas. John would call into the chippie on the way home, buy chips and I'd serve this repast with fresh crusty bread. Drink? Well in those days it was beer or sherry. No such thing as tinnies so I decided to get sherry from the barrel at the beer-off and accordingly got some old bottles, washed them out and put the corks on to boil clean.

Meanwhile we had an excited baby who was just about to go to bed in preparation for Santa's 1st visit. We had her on the bed tickling her and she was giggling when I smelled gas. The corks! I ran downstairs and found that the water had boiled over and put out the gas. I went to move the pan off the stove and it burned my hand something fierce. I turned to throw it in the sink but unknown to me, John was right behind me with the baby lying flat across his hands and I smacked the boiling hot saucepan straight into her face. What a nightmare. For the second Christmas of her life she was in hospital. Fortunately she was unmarked but it left me pretty scarred. Even after all these years that awful scene has lost none of its impact for me.

CHAPTER FOUR

OUR FIRST REAL HOLIDAY.

In those days there used to be a time - the last week in July and the first week in August - known as 'factory fortnight' in which a lot of industry closed for two weeks and folks took their holidays then. Adelina's where I worked didn't do this but John's firm Metallifacture subscribed to that holiday period. In 1961 I eagerly looked forward to this break. We hadn't got much money so a holiday was out of the question but we could go out as a family and enjoy a bit of leisure time in the sunshine. Taking Laura to the paddling pool in the Nottingham River Trent Embankment for example, or taking a picnic on the Castle Grounds. It was with a happy heart that I left work that Friday night and joked with the girls that I would think about them as I lazed about for the next two weeks.

I picked Laura up in high spirits, fed her sweets and tickled her tum all the way home as she sat in her pram. For the next hour, I was ignorantly happy and went about my chores with a light step. My husband was unusually late home considering his factory was due to close at 4.30pm that day and I assumed he had dropped off at the Lumley pub on the green to have what he called a 'swift half' with a mate or two. When he did finally come home he was stony faced and dragged his way into the house with his shoulders slumped. He looked grey.

"Awww duck, I don't know how to tell you." He spoke even before he was through the door.

"Tell me what?"

"I was robbed at work today."

For a second I stared uncomprehendingly at him.

"What? I don't....."

"Some bastard nicked my wages out of my jacket pocket."

"*What*?"

"I got my pay, all three weeks of it; put it in my jacket pocket and some cruel get nicked it."

"Did you get the police?"

"Yes, I called in on the way home but it was no use. I was one of the last to leave and didn't even miss it until I was halfway home. The factory is all shut up for a fortnight and we have to face it, the money has gone."

"What are we going to do?"

"The police have advised me to go and see the Social Security on Monday morning and see if they can help."

(Linger a little here and think what we, who were already so poor, had lost; imagine you losing three weeks pay today, there was - pro rata – no difference to what we had lost. Whichever way you look at it, it was a fortune. We never found out who did it. And I wish them harm unto this very day.....)

I raved at him for being fool enough to put the money where it could so easily be taken. But no amount of rage would bring that money back and reluctantly I returned to work on the Monday as usual leaving the baby in John's care. What else could I do?

We got no help whatsoever from the Social but a few days later, mam won over £100 on the bingo (an absolute fortune in those days) and never offered us as much as half a crown. I took my washing to the launderette the following week and called in on her. She was over the moon as she showed me the new corsets, underwear, coat, dresses and shoes she'd bought and which were now thrown carelessly over the back of her chair. She'd blown the lot. Our good close friends Jeff and Doris Marshall dug deep in their own pockets and gave us £2. Believe me, it was more than the proverbial widows mite seeing as how they had three small children and were every bit as cash strapped as we were. I have never ever forgotten that act of kindness. Life went on.

The following summer, I was able to persuade a reluctant John to take us on a much needed fortnight's holiday. He borrowed an ancient, tiny gas lit caravan from a friend of a friend and the deal included the owner taking us and fetching us back from Skegness but at great expense which had to be paid up front. Once again, I had little in the way of money and so it wasn't going to be the best of holidays, nevertheless I looked forward to it eagerly. On the afternoon of the very first day we had no sooner got there than Laura took ill with a painful throat infection and I had to call a doctor. Poor little soul cried piteously with pain and her temperature was sky high. The weather was glorious but all we could do was go out individually as the doctor had advised us to keep her indoors for the first week.

John found some friends in the next field and went out with them nightly whilst I nursed Laura. As she got better towards the weekend, the weather got worse and when she was able at last to go out, the heavens opened twice, once for four days and again for the last three! This holiday was to prove mam right she said; we should have gone to Mablethorpe! Naturally I had to stay in and look after Laura once my not now so beloved had gone out for the evening with his friends. He had recently had an expensive made to measure Crombie coat and wore it nightly that second week for the weather had turned very cold. One night making his way back to the caravan, he took a wrong turning in his tipsy state and fell into a ditch full of stinking black mud whilst wearing his new coat! I resisted the temptation to gloat, but only just.

With no 'Hyson Green' type shops to buy our food, we were at the mercy of the onsite shop and my purse soon emptied. One night I left the baby with John and went alone to the Embassy Theatre, entered the talent show, sang and managed to win it! The prize was a fiver I seem to think and it went a long way towards feeding us for the remainder of the holiday. The rest of the time I spent alone huddled up in the van as nightly the rain beat down incessantly. It was grim. There were a few short breaks in the conditions during the day in which we snatched walks along the beach and it was on one of these walks I overheard my first ever portable tinny transistor radio. I stopped dead in shock as it gave out the sad news that Marilyn Monroe had just died.

I recall dad often saying 'I'll be glad when I've had enough of this!' and I was more than glad I'd had enough of this holiday and was happy to be going home. I would forever say I had spent a month in Skegness one week! I packed and cleaned up after us and having paid in advance for the return journey, we waited for the car to turn up and fetch us. We waited and waited and waited...but he didn't show and we had no alternative but to take the bus back. The following year I vowed would be different and we would have a proper hotel holiday like normal people did. But it was to be a few more years before we managed to take our kids on holiday and this time we went to Butlins Holiday Camp. But meantime, every other holiday we had after that was spent at his sister's place in Barrington and I have some very happy memories of her kind hospitality in that beautiful part of the country.

There is one memory I have of one of those Cambridgeshire holidays... One year Iris took hers and my kids to a fete leaving John and I alone. We were sharing our bedroom with our two daughters so as usual there was a little something lacking on this holiday! It was a glorious day and we went for a stroll down to the Cam edge. We sat in the warm sunshine; the only sound the lapping water and the birds wheeling overhead. It was idyllic. We sat for some considerable time in peaceful isolation when the urge came upon us. Throwing caution to the wind we did as lovers have done since time began. It was heaven ....until I got bit, again and again, I didn't know what it was that bit me, but my backside was stinging something awful. I jumped up screaming and ran bare arsed through the orchard, into the bathroom and jumped in the shower. Red ants are not conducive to love making - especially when you are laid, albeit very tenderly - right on top of their nest.

Once we had got back home the clammy damp and the bouncy floor were not the only problems with our Durban Terrace house. Bearing in mind that these were very much pre fridge days, trying to take care of our food was a nightmare. There was no room in the kitchen for anything other than the small narrow workbench type table we had been given. This was pushed up to the huge yawning gap of the old fashioned range down which the wind screamed. It was at least a hundred years older than the Moffat Street monstrosity mam had lovingly Zebo'd to perfection. I had no such affection for the one in my kitchen and left it to its own rusty devices! There were a couple of rickety wooden shelves high up on the walls and these held all our pots pans and dried foodstuffs.

I first noticed strange noises and rustlings coming from the cellar almost immediately, well before we had even moved in. These diminished somewhat once we had the new floorboards in place but when we had moved in proper, it soon became evident we had mice. Not only did I learn of their existence but also where they lived. Having left a loaf of bread on the table when I went to bed one night, I arose the next morning to find all the soft inner bread gone and the remaining outer crust was covered in coal dust. Ergo the little sods lived in the coal cellar. Now, fond as I am of crusts.....

I bought a trap. That night I gingerly set it with a bit of cheese and nearly lost my fingers as it snapped down on me. I re-set it again and again until I finally got the hang of it and came into the sitting room and sat down. Within one split second there was a 'snap' sound and I went back again to re-load it. Caught in this evil trap was a tiny mouse, the spring had snapped shut across its nose and it was dragging itself in agony across the floor. I was hysterical with guilt; got a neighbour to sort it out for me and the trap went into the dustbin. I bought a second hand old fashioned green enamelled bread bin off the aforementioned Sneinton market and kept the other small amount of foodstuff I had in the living room cocktail cabinet ever after that. The thought of that poor little mouse still brings tears to my eyes.

The mice though were the least of my worries. The sagging floor was a living nightmare. Bearing in mind how wet and cold the house was and in those days winters were especially cold, we had a roaring coal fire going day and night. Now when we walked across the floor, the burning coals actually moved and this was one party trick I could live without. I had visions of the floor giving way whilst toddler Laura was playing on the hearth rug and of us all falling into the cellar and being burned alive. Someone told me of an official complaints department I could go to who had the power to order the landlord to rectify the fault. I seem to think it went under the umbrella of the Health Department, but I would stand correction. I went to see them, was invited to make an official complaint and did so.

The following week, a building inspector came to see me. I showed him how a few steps across the room caused the furniture to all but topple over and how the vibration affected the glowing coals. Looking worried he went down into the cellar, knocked bricks out of the dividing wall to gain access under the sitting room and inspected the floor above his head.

He was horrified. He said the fireplace was now resting on a few bricks and he could see the flames through them and the floor below was littered with fire ash. It could go at any time. I had many sleepless nights until I got a letter from the landlord and then realised I didn't know what a sleepless night was. He gave us a months notice to quit. I was frantic with worry and took the day off work to go and see the 'health department' and show them the letter. They would 'see what they could do'. A few days later a building firm turned up and hammered in 14 pit props under the floor and fireplace, levelling it out and firming it enough to make it safe.

We then got another letter from the landlord pointing out the houses were due for demolition in the not too distant future and so it was wasted money to spend any more on them and if I made any more complaints they would shut the house up again and we would have to go. I kept my mouth firmly shut from then on. I felt a continuing deep shame at having to live like this and likened it to an ant caught in a basin, no matter what I did or how hard I worked, I felt totally trapped. I wanted better for myself and for my family.

By now, as the result of hard work and long hours, my husband was the transport manager of his company and must have earned a relatively higher than average wage and we should not have had to live like that. Time and time again I tried to get him interested in buying our own home but he viewed a mortgage as a millstone around his neck much the same as I viewed his hard drinking to be a millstone around mine!

But no matter how bad our living conditions were he never seemed to want anything more for himself, me or our child. Provided he had his toast for breakfast, a cooked lunch at his mam's, a few nightly pints and the invariable – no matter how I tried to change it – supper of a cheese and tomato sandwich, he was content. Once he was behind his paper it was as if the world melted away and he saw and heard little else. Trouble was beginning to fester..... A man might gotta do what a man's gotta do but a little late in the day this woman began to develop a back bone and decided she had got to do what she had got to do......there had to be a way out of this poverty stricken nightmare of a life.

CHAPTER FIVE

GROMMAR.

I have already told you about my grandmother-in-law whom we all called grommar, who lived with May and George, she occupied the front room of the three storey terrace house next door to my parents on Bobbers Mill Road Hyson Green. She had once been tall and elegant but was now stooped, bony and thin with a mop of thick snow white hair which she caught up in a hair net and had the most enormous ears I have ever seen on anyone, before or since. This old gentle lady was treated badly by May and George. They had a TV by now but the only sight grommar had of it was as she trotted to the back yard lavatory having to pass through their sitting room and then if she lingered awhile standing behind her daughters chair to watch it, she was exhorted to go back to her room and close her door.

George unkindly called her Humphrey Bogart. May admittedly cooked for her but the meal was served on a tray in her own room and she was never permitted to sit at the table with them. I loved her to death and tried to look after her without upsetting the family but it wasn't easy. May resented her living with them but the irony of it was it was *grommar's* house. May and George actually lived with *her* but after so many years the lines had got blurred somewhat and grommar was unfairly considered the cuckoo in her own nest.

May and George had the backroom and at the first whisper of winter it was instantly bathed in the luxuriant warmth of a roaring coal fire courtesy of the free allowance given to all miners back then. Grommar's front room was deathly cold. Although George had this concessionary fuel, grommar was given one bucket a day and had to eke it out. Now, anyone who needed paying or if family and friends visited, they came straight off the street and through what effectively was grommar's' bed-sitting room letting out all the hard won warm air and letting in icy cold draughts in the bitter winters.

Without even a radio for company, the old lass sat silently watching folk pass by her window for years, thick hand crocheted shawls pulled tightly round her thin frame. Grommar complained to me one day how cold she was at night in bed and that year I bought her a beautiful warm pale blue woollen satin edged blanket out of Littlewoods catalogue for her Christmas present. She loved it but all hell broke loose when May and George saw it.

I loved this old girl. She was super sweet to me and many are the times she secretly gave me money to buy a treat for Laura. I in turn trotted off to the bookies and put her a bet on a few times a week, home permed her hair and also kept her up to date on what was happening within the family because for some unknown reason the family members kept things from her. But for me, she would have gone to her grave not knowing that she was about to become a great, great grandma. As it was, sadly, she died before that baby was even born. May and George would not permit her to go to our wedding and only now do I wonder why? As I had left the church en route for the reception, I had called in for her to see my finery and had given her my bouquet not wanting to see it wither. She stood it proudly on the piano in her room and there is remained until she died!

I am playing devils advocate here in saying that you had to see both sides of this dilemma. My mother and father in law were getting on a bit themselves now and wanted to be alone for what was probably the first time in their entire married lives but whilst ever grommar was there that was not going to happen. And anyway, as she rapidly approached her 90th birthday, where else could she go? There were no such places as rest homes for old folk back then and she had the constitution of an ox. She often said she would happily run to her maker if only to join her beloved son in Gods own heaven once she reached the age of 90, by which time she would have outlived all her sisters and friends, but I believed she would live to be one hundred and ten given half a chance and bloody good luck to her. (Her soldier son had died of pneumonia by the way, on the last day of the war when he was on his way back home.)

At the end of 1962 May and George asked us if we'd look out for grommar that year as they'd decided to go away and spend a few days over Christmas and the New Year with Brenda and David and their two grandsons in Newcastle and it meant leaving grommar alone for the first time ever. I told the Commodore band I would not be working over this period and John, me and Laura - a lively two year old by now - agreed to move in and look after grommar for the duration which we were more than happy to do.

It was to be one of the worst winters in living memory and it seemed that almost as soon as May and George had left for the station in a taxi that Monday morning, it was already proving to be a frosty Christmas Eve and with them barely out of sight, grommar fell ill. But not so ill that she would miss her nightly tipple in the Old General pub across the road. (And who was the Old General have you like me ever wondered? Well, I will let you into a secret; he was a well known simpleton by the name of Benjamin Mayo who lived in the city centre. The local folk had nick named him the 'old general' and he was much loved and looked after by the people of Nottingham so much so that when he died they named this pub after him.)

That night Grommar popped her head around the door and told me she was going to the pub.

"Oh grommar, you must be mad to go out in this. You really shouldn't you know, you're not too well and it's treacherous underfoot; the pavements are just sheets of ice and the weather forecast says it's getting worse."

"I'm a bit better now and I shall be alright, they'll look after me once I'm there don't yo' worry. Just nip across at 10 when thi' close if ya would and help me back over't road."

"Okay grommar, I'll fetch you back."

I smiled at her. My husband was already out celebrating Christmas with our friends so it looked like it was just me and my toddler for the night. She settled down to sleep on my chest in front of the luxury of a miniscule b&w TV set on top of which a tiny Christmas tree was colourfully blinking, I too settled peacefully to await our baby's first *happy* Christmas.

I must have fallen sound asleep and woke to the sounds of giggling as grommar came into the room. I can see and hear her now, she was unusually happy and jolly with two high spots of colour on her cheeks from the icy cold night or it may have been from the drink that had been pressed on her by the Old General regulars. She had on her long black coat

68

and around her head and shoulders wore her usual deep purple hand crocheted shawl.

"You forgot to come and fetch me didn't you, ya naughty girl," she said giggling and grinning, hanging onto the sideboard with one hand and waggling her finger accusingly at me with the other. Struggling to wake up, I mumbled my apologies and watched as she did a little jig.

"It's ok; two o' the owd men across the pub bought me 'ome."

She saw no irony in calling *them* old! She began to sing in a high tremulous voice;

I wouldn't leave my little wooden hut
For you...hoo.hoo..hoo..hoooo,
I've got one lover and I don't need
Two...hoo..hoo.hoo hooo.

The next morning, Christmas Day was grommar's 90th birthday and she took ill proper. We wanted to fetch the doctor but she would not have it. I cooked a chicken dinner and gave her some but she did not eat it. I tried to bring her into the warmer sitting room but she resolutely remained curled up in bed fully dressed, her blue blanket pulled tightly around her thin form. John was very fond of his gran and banked her fire up to never before seen proportions and the two of us danced attention on her all Christmas. By Thursday the 27th and with the festive season over for another year – new years day was not a holiday back then - John was back at work and I left Laura with my parents next door and went shopping on the 'Green'.

I chanced upon Peggy my old good Broxtowe friend who now lived in Pleasant Row further down the main road

69

towards the Goose Fair site. She was just shopping and as I had not seen her in years I invited her back with me to see my cute toddler. When we got back, I picked up Laura and went back next door to May's house. Peggy was alarmed at grommar's breathing and whispered she thought it was the 'death rattle'. This frightened the shit out of me since I had never heard the expression before. Despite grommar's protestations, I instantly went to the public phone box outside the Old General and called the doctor.

Peggy stayed with Laura whilst I went but left as the doctor arrived and had I known I was never to see her again, I might have taken my eyes off my lovely ailing grommar and lingered awhile to wave Peggy a last sad goodbye, perhaps from this perspective, I might even have given her a hug but in my *then* world, women didn't hug women and she would inevitably have pulled away and called me a 'soppy owd cah', so unknowingly I let her walk away for the last time....

The doctor examined grommar talking soothingly the while and then came into the kitchen.
"I'm afraid there's not much I can do," he said matter of factly.
"She's not going to die is she?" I asked, fully expecting him to laugh out loud at such a ridiculous statement.
"I have known Mrs Alcock for a very long time and she has had a long and happy life, she is comfortable, is in no pain but you must realise she is a very old fragile lady and yes, she may well die very shortly. I know only too well she has always said that she would live to be 90. It seems her words are rather prophetic."

A strange electric atmosphere seemed to descend and hover in the air and I longed for John to hurry back. I stayed close by grommar's side until he came home at gone seven and then, after putting Laura to bed, the two of us went into the front room, drew the curtains and kept a watch over grommar for several hours. At one point she asked for the overhead light to be put out as it was hurting her eyes and John lit candles. Her breathing was odd and laboured. It would rattle and then stop for what seemed to be hours then she'd breathe deeply again. At one point she roused and asked me;

"Will ya mek me a new dress eh Joycey?"

I was holding her hand, and squeezing it said;

"Of course I will grommar, as soon as you are well."

It was only later I realised that what she had said was 'would you get me *undressed* Joycey'.

Time ticked on and for someone who will happily 'run to her maker if only to join my beloved son in Gods own heaven', she didn't seem to be in any great hurry to get there and her dying was long and protracted. She would give what I thought to be her last gentle gasp, her breath leaving her body almost as a whisper and her hand would go quite still in mine. I knew she was gone...only she then snorted and took another huge breath. This happened quite a few times. It was the early hours of the morning before she finally took her last short shallow breath and it escaped from her lips in a long poignant sigh, her hand fell limp in mine. Oddly at that exact moment Laura screamed from her bed and John raced to fetch her downstairs. I know it sounds daft now but for both of us, this was our first experience of death and we were afraid to go to bed spending an appalling night trying to sleep in the easy chairs in the sitting room knowing there was a dead person the other side of the wall.

At barely dawn the next day we discussed what to do and decided not to spoil May and George's first holiday but to wait until they came home on the second of January before letting them know of grommar's death. Meanwhile, we phoned for the Co-op undertakers to remove the body in preparation for the funeral, the very thing we should not have done, since it turned out the old lady hated the Co-op with a vengeance! We weren't to know. For the next few days I walked about in a stupor so badly had grommar's death affected me and one day we were walking past a noisy party going on in a neighbour's house. I commented on the unusual din to my husband and he asked what did I expect on New Years Eve? I had no idea what day it was.

May and George came back in the New Year. May was upset that grommar had died at the only time she had ever left her. It did seem unfair. She asked did I want to go with her to view grommar's body before burial and I went. She looked so peaceful; her gnarled and bony hands lay loosely on a white satin shroud. May lifted her hand and went to remove her lovely gold wedding ring. It was a weighty Welsh gold broad band which must have been quite valuable. I begged May not to do it, seeing it as robbing the dead I suppose. May laid her hand back. Of course it took years for me to realise she would not have been buried with that ring still on her finger and at some point it would have been returned to May anyway.

Grommar used to tell me that I had to have another baby, that it was cruel to bring Laura up on her own, so when I found out a mere few weeks later that I was pregnant again, I kind of blamed grommar. (My knowledge of biology has improved somewhat since those days and I have veered back to the stork theory!) In the spring of that year, I had to give up the Commodore job as I was showing more than a little this time around and had quite a sizeable bump. Back then, the idea of proudly displaying one's pregnancy was thought to be vulgar and we coyly hid them behind voluminous and often twee maternity clothes. After a long hard winter, it was a long hot summer that lingered well into autumn and I lumbered through it getting bigger by the hour.

Laura was by now at not quite three years old, a beautiful child fond of rough and tumble play, in fact she was and still is a living tornado. She had a habit of running at me full pelt and jumping on my knee. I sat her down one day, put her head on my tummy and asked her what she could hear. She listened very carefully, her plump round pretty face gazing up at me. She said it sounded like a bath full of water. I explained that inside my tummy was a new baby who would soon come out and be her new brother or sister and the rumbling sound was the baby asking Laura to stop running and jumping on my tummy or she might hurt it.

She sat up, her eyes widened in wonder as she looked at my rounded stomach and asked;

"Is the pram in there too mummy?"

CHAPTER SIX

SANDRA'S STORY.

John's irritation towards anyone visiting our home even extended towards my own family. He was never enamoured of my mother but he even extended it to my other family members. My sister Sandra, (Muff! From her devotion to the TV puppet Muffin the Mule.) by now a 15 year old stunningly slim tall blonde, was courting an eighteen year old young man named Dereck. They regularly came to visit me. After a while, I noticed she was putting on weight and passed pointed comment on it in an effort to get her to tell me she was pregnant but she would not take the bait. I so wanted to help her but short of coming out and asking 'Are you pregnant'; I did not know how to go about it. On our return from that awful Skegness holiday, my first port of call had been to the launderette wherein my mother now worked. As I heaved my laundry bag full of 2 weeks washing into the corner shop, mam's first scathing words were;
"Ayyo seen ah bleddy Sandra?"
So she knew then.
"Mam, don't let it bother you, she's not the first and she won't be the last."
She stared blankly for a nano split second before realisation bit in. Her eyes flared thunderously, dangerously. You do not need to know the rest of this conversation as it will only reinforce what I have told you so many times before of my

terrible lifelong relationship with my mother, suffice to say she loudly and vehemently denied it. Every customer stood stock still in horror as she publicly upbraided me. I was all the effing cows walking to defame my pure as driven snow sister in this rotten way. I retorted on the back of her outburst that I would find out whether she was pregnant or not, as I would go across right now and ask her face to face.

I walked across the road and went into my mother-in-law May's house. I told her what had happened and well aware of my mother's violence, her eyes widened in fear. I went out into the back yard where I called Sandra's name. She came limping to the door covered head to foot in bandages having fallen off her bike and then I realised what mam had meant. I told her that I knew she was pregnant and had dropped her in it with mam. Her eyes filled with terror and she immediately panicked. I calmed her down, asked her how far along she was and she tearfully told me she was about 4 months. I told her that if mam started in on her she had only to come to me and I would have her stay at my house where mam could not get to her. I stressed this over and over until she understood there was *nothing* she need be afraid of.

I then returned to mam and told her that it was true and that she was four months pregnant and if mam laid one finger on her, she was coming to live with me. Odd, I could stick up for my sister where mam was concerned but not for myself. I further told my shocked mam I would be there rock solid for my sister. And I was. I gave mam time to get her head around what I had told her then held the shop for her whilst she went across and had a QUIET word. Within a few weeks and at mam's insistence, Sandra was hastily married shortly after her sixteenth birthday. I bought her a pretty pale turquoise suit for her to wed in, a cake to cut and helped her all I could. Mam and dad for the second time missed one of their children's weddings out of a sense of pique and again helped not one iota, although they came through in spades once the baby was born I hastily and happily add.

In the fullness of nine months, Sandra gave birth to her son. Mam in her usual domineering manner told Sandra her first grandson was to be named Gary. My brave sister Sandra called him Paul.

To begin with Sandra and Dereck had moved in with his mother in Palm Terrace Hyson Green but within weeks of getting married a house directly across from them came empty as a result of an old ladies death and Sandra's mother-in-law jumped in fast and persuaded the landlord to give it to her son. It was again a crumbling back street ruin but was, unlike ours, in much better condition and the rent was a paltry 11/- a week which back then was a fair amount of money for such a property. I felt the injustice of it, for if I had only that amount of rent to pay myself, I maybe could have stayed home with my delicate baby until she got on her feet, or even have worked part time.

After only a few months, Sandra was told her house was to come down and she was offered a council house in the, by now, far reaching council estates. She didn't want to go and there were many people willing to trade with her. Dot and Donny some friends of ours were first in line. Their three storey house on Fisher Street a few yards away from me was in a lovely condition. For some reason though, their private landlord would not permit the swap. In the meantime Sandra was offered two council houses which she rejected and that left her with just the remaining one since you had a choice of three. She still clung to the idea that she would rather stay on the Green and tried other avenues but it looked as though she was going to have to move to the final one they offered in Aspley.

One day as she was bemoaning her fate at having to move out of the district, on sudden impulse, I took it upon myself without reference to my husband to offer her £50 to swap with me. My husband was furious when I told him what I had done and ripped into me for spending *his* money in this way. I have to concede in those days £50 was a LOT of money, probably more than the deposit on a house. You have perhaps heard mention of Sheila and Clac in my books and that very same year they bought a 3 storey terraced house on Vernon Road Basford and it cost £250!

Sandra was not so fussed but her hubby jumped at the chance and reluctantly she agreed the swap. So as I neared the end of my second pregnancy I went to the housing office to finalise the Aspley swap and in the queue got chatting to a lady who had just bought her own house and was now bringing her council house key back. She painted a fairly accurate picture of how nice her place was. Again on impulse I asked the housing official if it was possible to have this lady's house instead of the Aspley one and he gave me the key there and then. I was all set to move to a nice clean modern house at 25 Winscombe Mount Clifton and my bump and I hurried home to tell all and sundry about my our new home.

The male reader might want to miss the next couple of hundred words as we go into the mysterious male excluded world of pregnancy. There can be few male or females who have not experienced or at least heard about women's strange fancies like chewing coal or eating earth during that nine month period but with my first it was out of season and wildly expensive strawberries; with number two it was wanting hazelnuts in the middle of the night and walking for miles but not until it was teeming down with rain; and oddest of all, whiskey drinking!! On the odd occasion my bump and I went out socialising, I drooled over the smell of whiskey and usually had a couple laced with lime (UGH!)

With my third it was anything sour, the sourer the better. One day strolling through the now long gone and still missed central market, I saw a display of plump lemons, I began to drool. I chose the biggest one I could find, proffered my sixpence and asked him to cut it in half which he did. Unable to resist one more second I sank my teeth into its juicy flesh. He all but screamed. Throughout my pregnancy each time I passed the stall he would take a lemon, cut it open *give* it to me free of charge but order me to eat it out of his eyeshot!

Get a few of us girls together at such times back then and out would come the stories of Dr Cochrane, breech births, baby turning and the art of predicting the baby's sex, the latter had always been a most popular pregnancy pastime, bearing in mind that the 60's held no such wonders as scans to make an accurate prediction. These women never needed such modern equipment. Various methods handed down from generation to generation were used but the one most widely practised was the one in which a sewing needle suitably threaded was held aloft over a bulging tum which had been modestly bared.

All eyes of this witch like coven of old and not so old wives centred on this steadily held needle as it began to spin. Its 'success' actually depended on who was holding the needle as to which way it would spin, anti clockwise did it for some and clockwise for others And one also had to take into account whether the person on the end of the needle was left or right handed since that also seemed to make a difference. In the fullness of time my turn came round and in the still silence all eyes watched as the needle began to move over my risen belly and soon the holder confidently declared the sex. It wasn't just the way the needle spun either, there were other ways to tell. I was told I had carried my first child in what was called the 'all round' way with no significantly noticeable bump, whereas with this pregnancy I had carried it all up front, ergo it was a different sex. What really cemented the idea though was the fact that either the medical staff had got the date hopelessly wrong or 'he' was late and it was well known lads were lazy! So a little lad it was then.

As with my first child though, to be on the safe side, I had a female name ready and waiting just in case. She was to be called Cindy and the original Joseph John was still in place for my expected male child. But this time around throughout the last nine months I had deliberately knitted or made only white green and lemon neutral coloured baby clothes. I was not about to make the same mistake again and end up with the wrong colour for the wrong sex. Oh how sensible it is today with no hard and fast rule of pink for girls and blue for boys anymore.

Towards the end of September 1963, there was the small matter of the Christine Keeler/John Profumo scandal and a report had been ordered by the government. It was due out the very night I was supposed to have had my baby. I was alone as usual, my beloved having gone to the pub and recall the night as being cold and wet, it was raining heavily in fact. By that time, I had a small second hand rented TV set and was glued to it. The eagerly awaited report was expected at

6pm, then 7, then 8 but it was nearer 10 before the damning report was finally released to the BBC. I don't know now why I was so interested, but towards 10 I had a need to use the toilet. Not wanting to miss the damning report I hurriedly traipsed out into the blackest of nights, the only light being that which trickled through from leaving my own kitchen door ajar. I pushed open the loo door. It was a horrible place and there was nowhere you could sit that you didn't get a drenching through the holed roof. As I turned to flush the loo, I heard a rustle coming from behind the bowl and staring up at me, teeth bared were the horrid red eyes of the biggest rat I had ever seen. Ugh! I moved so fast I half expected to go into labour there and then, only my 'he' baby had other ideas and was not about to appear for almost another 2 weeks!

On October the 7th 1963 this 'he' turned out to be another 'she' and whereas she had lazed away an extra fortnight snug and warm in my womb, now she was in a hurry and was as quick and trouble free to arrive as Laura had been the exact opposite. I barely made it to the hospital before she was washed dressed and in my arms. In comparison to the incredible smallness of her sister this robust not so little bundle was so fat in the face her eyes appeared as two slits and she looked like a Chinese baby. But her birth had been easy peasy! I recall lying in the ward wide awake all night long totally awe struck at the thought I no longer had **a** child, I had *children*, I was the mother of *two children*. It was an amazing realisation.

Having had a relatively easy time I was sent home into midwife care the very next day. John had no choice but to take time off work to help look after me for the then requisite 10 days bed rest. This meant him having to cook for and feed us, clean and tidy up after us, attend to Laura's mine and the midwife's needs and he was not at all au fait with this. I actually felt quite sorry for him, almost regarding him as another child. He had total charge of Laura who was by now quite a handful and there was also the not insignificant matter of our house swap which was imminent. There wasn't a whole lot of packing to do since we hadn't got a lot of anything *to* pack but nevertheless, there was the removal van to organise and he had to liaise with my sister Sandra, something he was even less comfortable with.

We had of course made the trek to see our new house as soon as we could, taking two buses to what I saw as the back of beyond countryside. The house was on a wide clean smart road in a block of four just before the bend. It had a tiny front garden and a large back one. There was a good sized living room with big wide windows we could open and which let in save fresh clean country air. The ground floor was of big black bitumen tiles that I polished until they gleamed; a beautifully large square kitchen whilst upstairs there was a separate toilet, bathroom and three good sized bedrooms. It was bliss. For perhaps the first and probably only time in my life, I took on some serious debt. I bought a red Formica topped tubular kitchen table and four matching red chairs with red and white plastic covered seats; a matching low slung kitchen cabinet with glass sliding doors decorated with cocktail glasses and wine bottles which were outlined in black and which had a set of drawers attached to one side and it stood on black splayed legs with brass ferules as feet. It was ultra smart. I also got a dining room set of sideboard, table and chairs and a neat little blue fabric suite of a small sofa and two easy chairs. I kept my new house spotless.

(One day shortly after we had this suite, Laura not much more than 3 or so took it upon herself to iron her dollies clothes and unknown to me fetched the iron in, plugged it into the mains, sat it face down on the chair cushion and went off to play! Ever after that, the burned cushion never saw the light of day again.)

Upstairs I would eventually put both children into one room but for now Laura slept in it alone. I wanted the very best for my children and bought them a white bedroom suite consisting of a small mirrored dressing table, matching chest of drawers and tall thin wardrobe. It was decorated with large, brightly coloured Mickey mouse and co transfers. It was innovative, funky and beautiful. (It's stood the test of time and I still have it and use it in this my 'office', though old Mickey has disappeared under a few tons of white paint over these many years.) For the first time in my married life I had a home of which to be proud. But debt takes paying for and I had no money coming in beyond my £6.50 a week housekeeping and a few shillings a week family allowance for my second child, there being nothing for the first. I had to find work and fast.

I saw an advert in the local paper for outdoor machinists. The firm was Morley and Kemp. I had worked for this company briefly before I had left to live in Birmingham, so they knew the standard of my work and readily took me on. I was loaned a huge Wilcox and Gibbs overlock machine which fitted nicely but obtrusively into the corner of my smart kitchen; a box full of every coloured cotton bobbins known to man and bundles of badly paid underwear to sew. Making up a dozen full underskirts paid 6/- about 30p today. I hated it. The bales of work were bought and fetched back once a week and the sewing of it was left by me until the very last possible minute and I usually did a weeks work in one day, racing to have it ready for when the man came. But once again, I had my finances fairly straightened out.

CHAPTER SEVEN

CINDY

Cindy whilst being the most contented of babies was not an easy child to feed. No matter how carefully I bottle fed her, stopping midway to 'burp' her before so very carefully and gently giving her the other half, she would 'projectile vomit' her entire meal every which way hitting wall, ceiling, fireplace and carpet with consummate ease. When all she was taking was a bottle of (say) 3 ounces of formulae milk, it was more than a little distressing to witness this and I worried myself sick. She gained weight but minimally. Then one dawn about a couple of weeks into our new home, I awoke with a start and realised she had not woken for her middle of the night feed.

That scene of that room, the bed, the way the sunlight streamed in through the window onto her blue carrycot placed on a chest of drawers, its hood drawn up high against the slightest possible draught, even down to the yellow nylon nightie I was wearing are etched into my mind forever. I dare not look into the cot, its foreboding ominous quietness leading me to believe her to be dead. I screamed John's name and he awoke with a start. In one leap he jumped from the bed and tore down the hood. She was sleeping peacefully, her round fat face wreathed in a secret little smile. She never woke again in the night. Her feeding problems remained though and at four months absolutely out of my mind with worry I went to see my doctor and told him I was taking her off formulae and putting her on solids. He sternly advised me against such a move and said it was on my head.

That same day I fed her a full home cooked dinner ground up into mush and she lapped it up and what's more, it stayed down. At the end of the first month I took her back to the clinic and the nurse told me she had gained almost a full lb. The doctor said I seemed to know my own baby but it was not something he would recommend to any other mum. But I had noticed she was not a baby for drinking. Whereas Laura would drink something every hour or less, Cindy would only take a sip. Today she is near on a size zero and healthy.

For a while, I became one of the ladies who gathered for coffee in first this house then that but it really wasn't my cup of tea and so I made a few good friends and left it at that. I had one neighbour of whom I was very fond. Her name was Margie and she lived a couple of doors away from me. She had a husband Frank and small daughter. Margie was comical but in a totally innocent way. She came into my kitchen as I was sprinkling flour onto a bucket full of mussels. Margie watched what I was doing, a puzzled frown on her brow and then queried it. I told her my mother in law swore that keeping and feeding them for a couple of days fattened them up. She said she had kept goldfish but never mussels! She was *not* joking.

One day she came in and asked me what size my windows were. Having just made curtains for this room I knew the measurements exactly and gave them to her. A few days later, she came to me again complaining I had given her the wrong measurements. Puzzled I got the tape and measured them in front of her. I was spot on. I learned that on the strength of my sizes, she had gone out and believing all the houses were built exactly the same, the windows would all be identical too and bought new curtains for her windows only to find them short by a foot or more!

She talked fondly of how her husband was a whiz in the home and could put his hand to anything. If I ever needed any hep, I had only to ask him and it would be done. The first time I went into her home I was amazed at what her hubby had 'done' for her. He had decided to make a 60's 'must have' serving hatch. He had knocked out a few bricks and a few more than he'd wanted had fallen out. As he'd tried to straighten the intended 2ft square opening, yet more had fallen.... Eventually it was about six foot square, a gigantic hole that let in all sorts of draughts. But bless, he tried. When their TV set, a tall boxed affair lovingly polished over several years, finally bit the dust, he saw no good reason to merely dump it and removing its innards, placed a wedding photo of them both on its slanted screen and turned it into the biggest photo frame I have ever seen.

Frank was not above pulling folks legs if he'd a mind to. He very kindly dug our back garden for us and it was huge so it was no mean feat. He then told my 'any sort of housework shy' husband he needed to set a lawn and to buy a grass seed named Emerald Velvet which was specially developed to grow sideways. Innocently he tried going into several garden shops to buy this grass seed until someone put him right. He did not see the funny side and carried on hating gardening...and decorating....and painting...and sweeping the paths...indeed anything to do with house hold matters.... I meantime became damn near an expert at anything to do with the new concept of D.I.Y, decorating, painting, mending fuses and even going so far as to put a spur from a power-point in our bedroom, pull it through to the other side of the wall, thus creating a spare and much needed one in the kids room.

Alma Phillips, another one of my neighbours turned friends, lived around the corner and had a huge boisterous family. We met through our kids being in the same class at school. The two girls became firm friends and so both Laura and Dawn were equally at home in each others houses. Her hubby Dennis was a born father with a 'the more the merrier' attitude to children and so her family grew and grew even encompassing girl triplets but he adored all his kids and was more at ease with them than with people his own age. No doubt about it, they were a lovely family.

Their back garden truly amazed me. Whilst mine had reverted back to waist high meadow since Frank had kindly dug it over and John had neglected it, theirs had not so much as one blade of grass grow on it, so well was it trodden by so many feet. As you can imagine, if I had a tough time with my finances, hers were horrendous. I helped as much as I could by making dresses for Dawn and by passing on all my kids outgrown clothes but it was a grinding struggle for her and every month her period due date was a nightmare in the waiting.

Having two small children meant a mountain of washing practically every single day. From the very beginning of my marriage I had carted bags of dirty washing on the bus from Hyson Green to the Radford wash-house like all the other women. I remember the first time I had done it and an old lass had come to me and said she thought I was a newly wed. I wondered how she knew and looked down at my shiny wedding ring and said something to the effect that its shine gave it away. But she replied that it was not the ring that gave it away but the state of my laundry. It was so obviously brand spanking new and just wait until it had whacking great holes in it like hers!

Then, once mam took the job at the launderette, I got it done for free or for very little money. But now that I needed it most, it was impossible to make the journey to either the launderette or the wash house with a baby and a small child in tow and I reverted back to the old dolly tub and ponch method favoured by the previous generations. After a year of the back breaking laundry routine, a distant relative of my husbands bought a brand new state of the art (then) Rolls twin tub and offered me her old single tubbed Hoover. I couldn't have been more pleased. What had recently taken hours now took about 5 minutes. I was thrilled with it and unlike its modern counterpart, it never needed any attention.....eventually though the outer casing rotted away but the motor still churned on and on.

As well as the people already noted I was also blessed with kindly neighbours either side of me and the road was a pleasure to live on. The cost of getting to and from work for my hubby was a serious problem. The bus could not get him there on time and as transport manager, he HAD to be there on time. He bought a motorbike and sidecar! It was a monster of a thing but cheap to run and sufficient for our needs. Laura by now was a delightfully beautiful child with long glossy curly blonde hair and a wilful manner that drove me to despair at times.

The sidecar accommodated her in the back seat and me and the baby in the front seat. Laura soon got bored on long journeys to (say) our annual trip to Cambridge and knew that busy fingers could soon release the back window from its moorings and almost weekly we heard it clatter away under the wheels of cars as she released it again and again. Bad enough in the summer, but absolute agony in the freezing cold winter and on one such journey headed as we were to Barrington, we had no choice but to abandon our holiday and return home. Times many my patient husband expensively replaced it only for her to do it again. Smacking her little hand made not the slightest difference.

I am a contradiction and nobody knows this more than me. I had either all the patience in the world for my kids as children or none at all. But idiosyncratic to the end, I hated my kids going to school and would have kept them home with me forever. But Laura had to go. She joined the Clifton Highbank Primary school in September 1965. She had settled well into her class and was as happy as Larry, skipping eagerly into school barely waving to Cindy and me as we stood at the gate and watched her go in. She was a bright little soul, smart and sharp as a needle. She had already begun to read at home and was ahead of the other kids. Oh I missed her. To begin with, I used to take Cindy for a walk in her pushchair round to the school at what I knew to be Laura's 'playtime'. I would shout her over and stand and talk to her until the bell went. But it seems the teachers thought it upset her and asked me not to do it again and I didn't but oh it saddened me.

Soon it was Christmas and five year old Laura came home from school asking could she please *please* **please** have the class hamster for the holidays and of course we said yes. Her daddy fetched him in the boot of our car and it was fun to watch him run round and round his little wheel. He had to be fed once a week on a Thursday Laura told us. He was dead within the week. The feeding of him was given out to the best behaved children in the class and Laura's day was Thursday.............Johnny's was Friday, Maisie's was

Monday.... I was literally in pieces at the thought that the poor little mite had watched us stuff our faces with festive fare whilst he starved to death. After the holidays I went into town to replace him for the children on their return. Even in the pet shop I burst into tears at what had happened. If the kids in school noticed they never said a word about the different hamster that awaited them on their return and in future years whenever the question of having a live animal during school holidays the answer was an emphatic no.

To this day my kids will tell you they never played truant once; they didn't need to as they had only to say they didn't want to go to school 'because'. Usually this meant they'd had a fall out with a friend and things were tough at school at that time I would tell them to have the day off and when they got back things would have calmed down and be different, and they usually were. In their years of schooling if they said they didn't feel well it was a great joy to me to tell them to stay home. Where other mums would moan about their kids getting under their feet, I would look forward greatly to the long school summer holidays. This does not qualify me for 'mum of the year' I hasten to add, far from it, I still screamed and yelled at them like banshee's! But these were without doubt my salad years and even way back then I was keenly aware of it....

CHAPTER EIGHT

MY NERVES KNOCK MY OPPORTUNITY!

I read in the Evening Post there was to be an audition for Opportunity Knocks the then only TV outlet for talent. I entered and won a place in the show. It was an exciting time for me but sickening too. I had a love for modern jazz and scat singing so when I tell you my absolute idol was Ella Fitzgerald it might give you an idea of what kind of stuff I used to do. So I was stunned when Hughie Green sent me a small packet containing a 45rpm record of the song he wanted me to sing on the show. The Surrey with the Fringe on Top! (??)

Singing to me is like painting a picture. This word needs to be gentled out of my lips; that one needs no less than a lung full of air to do it justice. There are some songs you can play with but others should be whispered almost reverently. Songs I loved to sing like Julie London's Cry Me a River or Ella's Every Time We Say Goodbye would have been my choice, or even Danny Boy for many has been the rowdy audience I have bought to their silent knees with my rendition of this beautiful classic song. But hey the show had to be balanced right?

I had to go to Manchester for the weekend and naturally had to go alone. I was to report to a hotel where a room was booked for me and had to take along a couple of what I thought to be suitable dresses which in any event I'd had to borrow. From there I was taken to the studio and had to go through the required musical paces and also model both dresses only to be told neither were suitable and one would be got for me from their own wardrobe. It turned out to be an odd looking thing of mustard coloured satin with a tight straight skirt overlaid with another shorter at the front and longer at the back flared one with a black satin lining that peeped through. Though it fitted me like a glove, I was not enamoured of it but in the days of black and white telly, the dressers knew their stuff and it looked really good on the screen. I was astonished to learn that the screen lied; the beautiful blonde hostess of the show wore a magnificent swimsuit like red sequinned costume. At one point she turned her back on me and I noticed it was crudely safety pinned at the zip where the fabric had given way but with all those dazzling sequins the camera could not pick up the pins!

I slept really badly that night dreading the ordeal to come and could not under any circumstances have faced the breakfast food I was offered the next morning and so went hungry for the whole time I was there. John arrived in his motorbike and sidecar about lunchtime on the actual day of recording. I didn't get to see much of him beyond a glimpse as I was put through my rehearsal paces.

Came the recording hour and the programme began. It used a tried and tested format of Hughie Green chatting informally with a member of the next contestant's family. Then, last on that show was me and I'd chosen my husband to do my introduction. As the 'Clapometer's' needle (a clock that registered the volume of applause in the studio - honest, that was what it was called!) finally stopped registering the audience applause for the previous artiste (it was a man who whistled his way through the second world war, mimicking the falling of bombs and the drone of the B 52's!). The format was for the camera to follow Hughie from the 'Clapometer' to a small side set.

This consisted of two chairs and a small table where John sat uncomfortably, albeit dressed in his latest made to measure suit, waiting for Hughie to join him. The camera would then swing onto the two men as they made the introduction and then onto me stood waiting on a set made up of wagon wheels. Hughie sat down and spoke to John. I wish I had a copy of that appearance. (There are none it appears as the TV Company used the video tapes again and again, over-writing the previous weeks show. Pity.)

It began badly as Hughie sat down and asked John about me. John froze solid, his tongue frantically flicking his dry lips and his eyes wild with fear like a rabbit caught in headlights as a racing car bore down on it. I was watching from the sidelines and this did nothing to inspire me. I became absolutely petrified! Hughie began by asking him something innocuous about me. After his question there was a long silence lasting at least an hour and a half it seemed as I watched and waited anxiously willing him to speak. Hughie tried asking the same question in a different guise but the answer was silence. Hughie quickly and expertly picked up on his fear and took over the introduction. Then the camera was on me. Automatically I began to sing merely paying lip service to a song I could give nothing to. Then, quite suddenly I found I was at the end of my chance. Instead of waiting for my studio applause on the 'Clapometer', in sheer panic I raced off the set and collided with the startled TV crew as the cameraman vainly tried to keep me in his sight. Needless to say I came nowhere and returned home. The offers of work came flooding in...all one of them and that was to join a choir in West Bridgford. Ah well, back to the

Morley and Kemp overlock machine in my kitchen. However, almost immediately they ran short of work and my machine lay idle for a few months. I had to find work again and fast, but with two small children.....?

Disco was just coming into play and the mini was at its height. Literally! The housewives of Clifton were not about to be left behind in the fashion stakes and the hems began to rise. But money being tight for everyone in those days, there was no money for the new styled mini dresses and the ladies compromised by taking up their existing dresses. Only trouble was, the in fabric in those days was Crimplene a thick non iron man made cloth that did not take too well to being taken up four plus inches! They looked awful and I must have properly shortened by cutting and hemming at least one dress for every woman on our street. In retrospect even a few pennies from doing this would have helped but the idea of charging someone I knew for such a service was abhorrent. I did it for free; it would never have even entered my head to ask for remuneration. I also got a reputation as someone who would at the drop of a hat make you a dress to wear for (often) that very night.

It was not possible to leave two kids and go out full time and after adding travelling time to the day it meant there was very little profit in going out to work at all. I had a friend who lived close by. Sheila had six small children and she too was in the same financial boat as me. Out shopping one day, I noticed our local Woolworths had a sign up for a shop assistants position. I went in and asked could I work part time? I was told no. On the way home I had an idea and went to see my friend. Laura was by now well settled in school and if Sheila had my baby, I would have all her kids and we could do this job between us IF I could persuade the manager to allow it.

I could and I did and the two of us did one job and we shared the money. I worked the mornings and she worked the afternoons and the only fly in the ointment was the sheer noise of all those kids during the school holidays. But it worked fine until she took ill. She discovered a lump in her breast and within weeks had left those six children motherless. Once again I began to take work from Morley and Kemp but it was hard and time consuming. The only reason we outdoor workers had the work in the first place was because it was so badly paid the factory workers had refused to do it.

That winter, John finally got rid of the old motorbike and sidecar, buying himself a small white van. Since it was only a two seater, the kids used to sit on two small children's chairs in the windowless back! I have to wonder now how on earth they kept their balance as we went around corners. Mind, there was precious little traffic on the roads then compared to today and he was a good steady driver.

One of our close neighbours was a man of whom it was said locally 'One of his work stamps is so rare it's worth more than a penny black.' He did not like work and so simply didn't do it and he and his wife and kids lived in comparative comfort off the backs of the other hard working souls on the street by claiming dole money. During the summer months he also lived an extra good life off the added income provided by a couple of caravans he owned that were sited in Skegness and let out to holiday makers. He was not a popular man as I am sure you can imagine. His hobby was tinkering with old cars, several of which he had lined up on the street. Since he lived on a corner, the untaxed and often un-wheeled bangers stretched for about a hundred yards round the corner and so made parking difficult for anyone else.

By now most of our neighbours had a little car of some sort and since such ownership was very expensive in those days, liked to have them close by so as to keep an eye on them. With the cars already in situ across the street from us, we had to park on another street. Times many my husband would come in sopping wet and half frozen having had to walk several hundred yards in the driving winter rain whilst the cars opposite continued to rot. John could not reason with anyone. It was just not his wont. I begged him to go across and remonstrate with the man and get him to move some of them to allow us to park. But he wouldn't. Instead he began to shout threatening remarks across at the house when he had a belly full of false courage after drinking all night and the neighbours began to talk. I lost some considerable respect for my husband at this point.

Aware that John had been an A.B.A (Amateur Boxing Association) champion a few years previous and could well have harmed this man if the parking problem got any further out of hand, I took it upon myself to go and see the housing department and ask had they a house with a garage? They were like gold dust I was told but they did have one, it was on Whitegate Vale and it was awful, was £1 a week more expensive but it had the garage and a drive and so we took it. I did not like this house one iota and in the moving, lost a little more respect for my husband. It was dark, dank from the concrete outer pebble dashing and had the most ridiculous additional window high up on the sitting room wall. It was too high to see out of, ditto to see in and looked stupid no matter how I tried to dress it. The kitchen was tiny and there was no room for the industrial sewing machine so I had them take it back. That was the only good thing about the move.

Now I had no choice but to go out and get a proper job and the only job that paid me well was machining. But with the added expense of the house change, additional rent and van costs to consider, I started to look for work immediately. Since there were no factories close by, it meant daily commuting into the city. Laura was moved to the little school down the road from us. Once she was established and settled, I began to look for work again. I found a good well paid job in St Mary's Gate in the Lace Market. This area is without doubt one of the most ancient and pretty of this city. It has some truly breathtaking architecture, although it's slowly and steadily being eaten away by the modernisation that's taking place in the city. Chambers Bros on St Mary's Gate was in an ornate pretty honey coloured building. The boss understood the pressures on women with families and I was permitted to work hours to suit my commitments. All I had to do now was settle Cindy in somewhere. I found a first class, albeit expensive nursery at the bottom of Green Lane and I was up and running.

The first day after taking Laura to school I took Cindy to her nursery. I was worried sick expecting her to cling to my skirts in fear but as soon as we got through the door she toddled off and within seconds was playing happily with the other children and didn't even turn to wave goodbye and I found my bottom lip trembling. I could not help but recall my first day in school and the misery I had felt being unable to relate to the other kids. I still wonder to this day why that was.

"First day?" asked a pretty young woman at my side. She had dark hair and a trim slim figure.

"Yes, I hardly slept last night for worrying but I can see I needn't have bothered." I sighed, adding "why do we teach our kids to walk only to watch them walk away?" She laughed.

"You should have been a writer..."

We fell into step and walked to the bus stop. I discovered her name was Rose and she also worked as a machinist in the city, she had a small daughter Mandy at the nursery. She told me her story biting her lip to hold back her tears as she spoke. Her adored husband had walked out and left her for another woman a few weeks previously and she was in dire straits both emotionally and financially. By the time we reached town we knew all about each other and began what was to become a lifetime's friendship. Sometimes her little girl stayed with me overnight giving her mum a chance to go out and start her life again. Sometimes my two girls stayed at Rose's house and John and I got to have a night out. And sometimes we two girls went out together and there are a couple of stories I can tell you about those nights.....maybe later.

I settled in well at Chambers. The supervisor was Elsa a tall thin elegant lady with beautiful thick honey blonde hair and an adored daughter Frances. The work-girls were to become almost like a second family to me and were a varied bunch; Dolly 'call me what you want, just don't put 'old' in front of it', Sheila of the booming voice and matching booming personality, Hazel who was as timid as a little mouse, June FoxSmith my immediate sewing neighbour, Gladys and her daughter Muriel (Muriel went on to become my youngest daughter Zoe's godmother), Vera, and one lady

Jess Maltby who was to become another lifelong friend and whom I lost only very recently at the grand old age of 96. These women became true friends and confidants in a way I had never known before. I worked happily at this firm for quite a few years and have kept in touch with a few of them for many more. They have been spectators to the pages of my very varied life. Within a few weeks I was to need them in a not very nice way.

I had a pregnancy scare and Cindy was still not much more than a toddler. The innovative birth control pill I had been using since her birth was in its infancy but it had largely set women free from unwanted pregnancy though there was a stubborn streak of women who were too scared to take it. But even for the rest of us, in those days we were only permitted to use it for a short time and then had to come off it and find other contraceptive means, only going back on it again at your doctor's discretion. I had been made to come off it a few months before and now here I was worried sick again.

Contraception was moving forward but still had a way to go and the thought of yet more responsibility of another unplanned pregnancy weighed heavily on me. As it turned out, it was simply a late period but it spurred me on to go and see my doctor to discuss the limited contraceptive options. He told me I still had a few months to go of the requisite break before I would be allowed back on the pill but there was the Dutch cap - a messy affair - or the new 'coil' which was gaining in popularity. I was referred to a specialist docter to have one fitted. It cost £5, a not insignificant amount of money back then. Still, for the sake of my peace of mind....

A few weeks later, I was on my way to work and had settled into my seat on the bus. As I had left the house, the postman had given me a bunch of letters and I opened them now. Gas bill, council rent increase, health service....HEALTH SERVICE? It was from the Nottingham City Hospital and told me an appointment had been made for me to be admitted to the gynaecological ward next Wednesday at 10am for a cone biopsy procedure and I would be required to stay in hospital for a few days. Immediately I began to worry, no that's not quite right, I was puzzled more than worried. I had no idea what a cone biopsy operation was and thought it could only be related to the fact that I had not gone back to the hospital after the birth of Cindy for a post natal appointment. But what with moving from Hyson Green to Clifton, setting up a new home and looking after two children it had slipped my mind and I now grew worried that I might be in a bit of bother with the medical department.

I am not one for going to the doctors unless it's something that really bothers me. Hence a few years ago I made an appointment with my local surgery and Doctor Alexander greeted me with the words

"Oh hello....new patient?"

"No, I have been on your books for twelve years."

"Well, I have not seen you before."

"No, I keep away from you unless I need you and I haven't needed you."

"Wise woman" he replied laughing.

But though I was not a regular visitor for my own health, I did visit the baby clinic often, eager to keep my children healthy and surely the doctor would have told me if there was any sort of question about my own health?

By the time I got to Chambers Bros I was no wiser. I showed the letter to the girls at work and we chewed it over. It was Jess Maltby who put me on the right road.

"I don't think its anything to do with not going for your post natal. Cindy is eighteen months old isn't she?"
"Well, yes."
"Believe me; they'd not bother you after all this time. It could be some sort of check up linked to having that coil fitted."
Relief flooded through me.
"*Of course!* I think you are right, its probably to check that's its been fitted correctly."
Why hadn't I thought of that? Jess went on;
"Who did you go to see when you had it fitted?"
"Dr Eden."
"Ring her and ask if it's anything to do with that coil."
I went to Elsa, showed her the letter, explained my problem and asked if I could go out to the phone box across the road? She kindly allowed me to use the firm's phone. I found the number in the book and rang the surgery. It was Doctor Eden herself who answered. I explained who I was, reminded her of my visit to her to get the coil fitted and told her of the mystery appointment. There was a brief silence then
"Didn't you get a visit from your doctor?"
"No."
"Didn't you read my letter?"
"What letter?"
"I sent you a letter."
"I got no letter."
There was again a silence.
"Just hang on a minute will you?"
I heard her apologise for the delay to someone in the room and then heard drawers being opened and closed.
"Hello? Oh Mrs Blacknell, I am so sorry. The letter to your doctor is still here, I have forgotten to post it."

(There had been a witness to this whole conversation. The person the doctor had apologised to was Alma Phillips who hearing my story of the coil had gone to get herself fitted for one and was in Dr Eden's surgery when I had phoned.)

My head reeled as she explained over the phone that before fitting the coil she had been required by the health department to do a pioneering smear test on me and it was positive for pre cancer cells. Instantly even as I sat at the boss' desk in his empty office, I was leaving my family motherless and began to plan my funeral! That is me, always looking on the bright side of life! (Sounds like a good title for a song!) I staggered out into the workroom and my face must have betrayed me as the room went silent but for the clatter of the machinery belts. I walked in a daze into the rest room followed by the entire workforce and lit up a fag with shaking hands. I told the girls and they listened in horror. Pre cancerous cells, the only word there of any significance was the word Cancer which was a death threat and it was on *my* head.

That night, my own doctor came to my home to see me and swore he had written to me and I had just not got the letter. Whatever. The next few days were a nightmare and John and I clung to each other in mortal fear. Then it was Wednesday 'D' day and he took me to the City hospital with both kids in tow. The staff allowed them to accompany me to the ward and to stay a few minutes as I settled in. Then they took their leave and I watched as he left the ward, Laura in her blue coat, her small hand in his and Cindy in her red siren suit carried in the crook of his other free arm. I was convinced I would never see them again. I was home on the Friday and returned to work on the Monday. I explained to my workmates that I had been warned any more children I might have in later years would have to be born by caesarean section but hey, I had enough kids and was never going to have more anyway...oh girl, never say never.....

I may have only worked part time, but it made no sense to me not to put my back into the job and earn as much as I could in those hours. I have to admit though it was hard work. In the winter, I was up before it got light and it was dark by the time I got home. The house was very damp and icy cold in the absence of central heating. I would pick the girls up from school and nursery, hurry them home, put them in the kitchen with all four gas jets on to keep them warm, get their pyjama's and put them over the plate rack on the stove to warm through, tidy up the kitchen from our hasty breakfast and get them some tea on. Whilst they ate, I would hurriedly clean out last nights ashes from the grate, get the coke fire going again and tidy up the living room. Then go back into the now nicely warmed kitchen to prepare mine and John's dinner and whilst that cooked, get the girls bathed and ready for bed. Then they would go into the warm living room and sit and watch TV or play for a while.

By the time John came home they'd be tucked up snug and be sound asleep, his dinner would be on the table. Then I would tidy away the kitchen mess, get the girls clothes out ready for the next morning and finally fall into an armchair for an hour or two's TV. By this time, he would be fast asleep, his feet stretched out to the warmth of the blazing fire, his head resting on hands crossed over his chest.

One night is forever etched into my mind; it was winter and I had earlier come home in the late afternoon, fetched the children from nursery and school through the wretched weather of driving icy rain and, already dog tired from my days work, had gone through the above mentioned ritual which involved looking after the kids, cooking dinner and doing housework before falling fast asleep. I awoke with a start and looked at the clock. It was just after 9pm. John was still snoring gently. I looked across at my husband and it was as if I had never seen him before. A strange thought came into my head. Is this it? For the rest of my life, is this really it? Will I dash home night after night forever till death us do part and go through this routine just to sit by the fire and snore? Is what I have behind these four concrete walls really all there is to my life? Five days a week hard factory graft with only the Saturday night out in the pub with the lads wives for company, I told myself I was twenty six years old and this daily back breaking boring grinding poverty was all I had, all I could see me ever having. I vividly recall my marriage ending that night.

CHAPTER NINE

THE MUSTERS

My friendship with Rose continued to grow and we began to go out together sometimes. Such nights were gloriously innocent and were an escape valve for Rose and in retrospect I suppose for me too. I remember one night we went to the Ram's Head on Mansfield road. I don't know now why we wound up there, it must have had some appeal but I don't recall what. It was decidedly lacking in atmosphere due to it being totally empty save for the two of us. We sat for a while and resolved to finish our drink and go elsewhere. At that precise moment the door opened and a room full of men tumbled in. It was a 'headed for the coast' men only weekend coach trip. As I recall they seemed to be mainly old men, but when you are in your mid twenties, anything over thirty five **IS** old. One of them got up on the stage and took to the piano. He was surprisingly good. Inevitably we got chatting to a few of them and at one point I kicked Rose's foot under the table and gave her the 'look'.
"We are heading off shortly ourselves," I said, "We have a booking in London for the BBC to film a show." I straight facedly told them. Their ears pricked up.
"Oh, what do you do?" asked one.
"We are members of the Ivy Benson all girl band. We both sing and Rose also plays the trumpet."

I looked across at Rose whose face was stony giving nothing away unless you could count her eyebrows which were raised by several inches.

"Give us a song then."

(Have you ever heard Rose sing? Ohhh, I have!!!!!)

"No can do I am sorry, we are under contract to Ivy and if she found out we would be sued. Do you know the contract is so tight we could not even sing at a family gathering?"

Word had spread and by now we were the very centre of attention and they kept firing questions at us and contracts or no, kept begging us to entertain them.

"Well I suppose we could do just the one."

Rose's eyebrows disappeared behind her ears! I dragged her onstage and asked the man to play Hey Big Spender.

With her arm pushed high up her back, she came through with flying colours! The two of us belted out that song as though we did it professionally every night with an all female band! Although I say it as shouldn't it was a remarkable performance. The guys raised the roof with their enthusiastic applause. We signed several beer mat autographs, drank up, refused all other offers of further drink and took our leave in a dignified manner. It was only when we got outside that we literally collapsed on the car park and peed ourselves laughing.

Thus I had started to make a new life for myself and it was on a Friday night out with Rose again that I discovered the Musters in West Bridgford. The hotel was owned by the Harvey family, namely Norman, his wife Iris and his two sons Charles and Rex. Norman was a huge man. His wife had been a nursery nurse, a beauty in her day and with her trim figure and long blonde hair was still worth a second look, even as a mother of the two teenage boys. The Musters had started as a simple small hotel but once Norman had hit on the idea of opening a cabaret room it took off like a rocket. Very much the in place at that time, it was an exciting, smart - if somewhat crowded - venue that began to attract people from all over the county. The long suffering neighbours thereabouts would tell you it had non stop loud live music often until well after midnight even though the official closing time was about 10.30pm I believe. As the houses nearby became empty or came up for sale, Norman snapped them up and added them to the Hotel until it was quite a sizeable place.

The cabaret room was glitzy, glamorous and totally professional. Its small stage was to be graced by some of the finest keyboard players in the country never mind the county. I recall gifted pianists Burt Hartley, Austin Payne, Johnny Mays and Gordon Verne. They also had a succession of talented drummers whilst I was there and again I can only recall a guy named Johnny who for some unknown reason they called Elvis and a guest drummer whose name I am sure a lot of you will remember, the legendary Nolly Buck.

Got to side step here and tell you of a little story about Nolly; He was married for a long time and I am sure he had two children whom he had bought up to or near adulthood when he fell for the charms of another lady who was much younger than he. There was to be no turning back and he made his life with this girl who in the fullness of time, the fullness of nine months actually, bore him twins. The last time I saw him he was living on a boat at Hazleford close to the Star Ferry pub.

He was quite a man. I recall our last conversation when he told me about his(second wife (?) and the twins. He told

107

me all about his boat and invited me to go and see him. He described how he was moored on the bend of the river and had rigged up the sound of the Queen Mary fog horn and relayed it through loudspeakers on his deck. As twilight descended and turned into evening and the mist was rising and thickening, he waited until he could hear the tiny chug of a small boat nearing the bend and then play the 'BOOOOO-- -OOOOOM' sound full blast and the hapless boat owner would shit himself as he rounded the bend. Oh Nolly you were an idiot! Again, where are you now?

Back to the Musters; the show was run by Cliff Worral for a while who was a smart bow tied singer/compere though at one time he fleetingly gave way to Roy Marsden, he of the velvet voice and classy stage presence. He stayed but briefly and went onto the ultra smart Parkside club a stones throw away and yet a world away from the old Moo Cow just around the corner. At the Musters it was the done thing to offer the mike up to anyone who wanted to have a go and with superb backing like that, I wanted to have a go. I walked out that night with the job of resident singer for three nights a week, 8 to 10.30pm.

*Do remember I had two children and their welfare was paramount to me, they were **never ever** cast aside, wherever I was to go in life, I held my children's hands and took them with me. I advertised locally for a baby sitter and along came one Elsie Seagar a gentle elderly lady who lived just around the corner. She was a little gem and we could totally rely on her. I paid her £1.50 a night which was a lot of money then. The kids loved her and she was our help for quite a long time. But once we moved to the Whitegate Vale house, mid* *week baby sitting was more difficult. John had not wanted me to take the Musters job but for once I put my foot down and reminded him that he had gone out practically every single night alone since we got married and I had sat with them night after night without complaint, it was time he did his share and to be fair he did it for a couple of nights a week without any problem.*

Norman had a brother Roy whose claim to fame had been the time he had spent in the states as a young man following no less an icon than Louis Armstrong. These two brothers did not get on too well and there were some spectacular and very public verbal rows between them. Roy lived close to the Musters in West Bridgford and Norman and his family lived with his father in the family home where Norman and his brother had grown up. It was right on the river just a stone's throw away from the main Trent Bridge. It had a beautiful garden fronting the river and Norman had quite a big boat tied up there. The house was a stunning place but sadly due to the frenzy of building there has been in this city the last couple of years, that lovely house is no more.

Often after the Musters shut at night, Norman would hold court and have a lock in until the early hours. I was not and never have been a drinker so there was nothing to keep me there and I would go home despite pleas to me to stay. But on other occasions, he would tell staff and hangers on to pile in our cars and follow him down into the town and we would visit the Pigalle or the Hippo nightclubs. These were fun nights and often Norman would foot the food and drink bill for the whole entourage.

There were some good names appeared at the Musters and in particular I remember Les Dennis, Diana Dors, Ronnie

Hilton, Mick Miller, Bernard Manning, Ronnie Carol and amongst many women, I particularly remember Anita Harris. She was very glamorous and professional and I was merely a gauche housewife who could sing a bit. I loved her gowns and envied her long hair which she advertised as being the longest in show business. Closer inspection revealed it to be a hair piece! But if you were looking for glamour, you needed to look no further than the 'Forthcoming Attraction' poster on the billboard at the foot of the stairs leading to the cabaret room. It showed an artiste or 'act' as the colloquialism would have it, a guy called Johnny Peach beautifully dressed up as a female impersonator. He was due the week Cliff went on holiday, so I took over the compering.

Wanting to look my best for Johnny Peach's opening night, I took myself off for a rare visit to a hairdresser. In the mid 60's hair styles were big affairs and involved having a perm and getting it set into hundreds of big bouncy curls that framed pretty faces. (Farah Fawcett?) Oh the style was to die for. I'd be in my mid twenties I suppose and expectantly went off to one of the best hairdressers in Nottm and asked for this style and the famous blonde colouring of the aforementioned Charlie's Angel. They duly set to work and several hours later, I looked into a proudly held mirror and saw her 'tongue in cheek' version of the style which on me was a fine Busby of yellow frizz approximately 2 ft in circumference! I looked a complete and utter prat as if I was wearing a large yellow fluffy hat on my head! It was horrendous and had cost something like an astonishing week and a half's wages. I was so stunned I actually tipped her, came out of the salon and amid a thousand surprised glances not one of which was of admiration, I scurried home. I felt the affro hair style had been invented for me! That night I had to go to work with this horrendous halo of kinked perm. I was well established by now and the punters and staff commiserated with me.

Johnny Peach was fresh new and glamorous and was topping the bill for the whole week. I was more than ten years further on from the thick red waxy lipstick of my first kiss but I had learned nothing about make-up in that time and apart from a scrape of lipstick, albeit it a new Ponds one romantically called Dreamy Pink and a brush full of frothy black mascara raised from a block with a bit of spit and a lot of effort, I wore little or no make-up not ever seeing myself as pretty or even attractive. I envied beautiful women their wolf whistles, the only ones I got were those I 'borrowed' when I was in their company!

*(And for all you men out there who may be reading this book let me tell you something about women that might gain you some brownie points; **all** women want to look beautiful for their man. It's nothing to do with ego and everything to do with being in love. In all my life via two husbands neither of them ever said I was pretty, beautiful, gorgeous, glamorous or lovely, not ever and its something we **NEED** to hear from the man we love, even if a glance in the mirror tells you it isn't true. I was once told grudgingly by my ex husband that he supposed I was attractive...oh thanks a bunch.)*

But all that was to change that night. Johnny Peach was my first experience of working with what is commonly called a drag act. I was to find out he was a caring lovely man. We shared a dressing room and chatted a little before I bought him on stage and he absolutely flattened that audience. For well over an hour, he sang, told jokes and fooled around with them. Man he was so good. And his dresses, oh those dresses.... He had them made in London and I am sure they would have even been coveted by Danny La Rue, he of those wonderful sexy gowns. Coming off the stage at the end of that night, I bemoaned my new hair do as I shrugged into my coat prior to going home. He took my shoulders and steered me gently towards the harsh light of the dressing room mirror where he studied my face carefully and said;

"You annoy me; you have everything I ever wanted in a woman. You have beautiful big brown eyes, a lovely flawless complexion you do nothing with and a fabulous figure that you cover up with a shapeless sack..."

Hey, let's back up here a minute, what did he say? Bloody marvellous the only man ever to tell me what I ached to hear even though I would not believe it to be true anyway, was a female impersonator!! Ah well, any port in a storm.... He continued:

"Let me make you up and show you just what you could really look like."

I have to admit, I was so used to thinking of myself as a plain Jane I could not for the life of me see what he meant.

Johnny was nothing if not professional and the dressing table was littered with dozens of boxes of Max Factor stage products. It was perfectly natural for him to apply thick heavy foundation and stage make-up in differing bright colours that he managed to subdue, turning himself into a stunning beauty. He also wore huge false eyelashes, black spiky things that were long enough to sweep cobwebs from the ceiling. I balked at the thought and flatly refused but he was not about to give up.

"Well let me just do one side of your face," he pleaded with me in his soft gentle voice, "and I absolutely promise you will love it and you can wash it off if you don't like it." Again I refused and pointed out I had to get home. "I'll give you a lift if you let me do your face. It will only take a minute or two." I sat down.

What he did next is legendary to all stage people who know me and him. He tastefully made half my face up, added one false eyelash, shaded my brown eyes with soft misty eye shadow, lightly brushed my cheeks with rouge and showed me my new face. He had somehow kept the make up to a bare minimum and I could not believe what was staring back at me from the mirror. I begged him to do the other side. The problem of my hair was solved when he chose one of his blonde hair pieces which he clipped onto the back of my head. He combed a little of my frizz over the top and pinned the rest of it out of sight beneath the tumbling curls of the hairpiece. I looked wonderful. He let me borrow it and told me where to go and buy one which I did the very next day.

I am certain some of you ladies will recall a little old lady who had a stall on the Central Market and who used to sell designer clothes off for a few pounds. She had a large audience of would be buyers and she would almost conduct an auction by holding something up and in a tiny tremulous voice ask for bids on it. I paid her a visit. Hanging on the outside of the stall were dozens of beautiful evening gowns made by well known fashion houses with names like Jacques Vert and Mary Quant. Such dresses had a limited market. I mean in those days how many women would go to places grand enough to need such finery? Because of this, the prices were ridiculous. This one was thirty shillings, and that one a quid.

I bought a 'to die for' Dior apple green knee length gown made of the sheerest chiffon with a plunging neckline and a short skirt overlaid with even finer chiffon. Another was a full length Jacques Vert model skin tight pale turquoise one made up of thousands of yards of tiny ribbons stitched every which way. (I have included a photo of me wearing it.) They were stunning and fitted me like the proverbial glove. That night when I walked in decked out as per Johnny instructions and wearing the turquoise gown, the response was astonishing. Johnny proudly said I was a fast learner and then set about re-naming me. With his help, Joyce Blacknell became Joy James that night. Norman told me to go to a professional photographer and he would pay for me to have pictures taken of my new look which he would put in the showcase at the Musters Club. And I did.

I will never ever forget Johnny's kindness. Through him I had become a new woman and found the answer to my hair and beauty problems. Ever after, every glam piccie of me in my books shows me wearing hair pieces or a wig and long false eyelashes, so from that night on I have him to thank for the fact that when I go to bed at night there is always more of me on the dressing table than ever gets in bed!

Over time, I got to know this entire family pretty well. Norman liked his drink and so did Iris but I would not call them drunkards by any means. Although Norman could get uproariously drunk and many was the night he'd stage his own show, much to the delight of the audience, by jumping on the stage at 10pm and announcing in no uncertain terms that the club was now closed for the night, further, he'd, not too politely, tell the punters to clear off, occasionally going so far as to switch out all the lights and thereby plunging the place into darkness. On more than one occasion he sacked his entire workforce of bar staff, musicians and ditto the artiste bought in at great expense for the week. The next day, nursing a throbbing head he would frantically run around mending fences and setting everyone back on again and in some cases at double the previous pay!

You'd think it would alienate the customers who very often were forced to leave their newly bought drinks behind. But far from upsetting them, they were rather fond of him and came back in droves eager to see if he could get any worse. After getting free drinks for those left behind on the previous altercation, the punters stayed hoping the pantomime was to be repeated and on many future occasions, it was. He was a pussy cat to me and treated me with reverence and kindness and often took me in his Rolls Royce to Clements music store in the city centre and bought me sheets and sheets of music, lots of which I still have. I had also known him put his hand in his pocket and give me a little extra to get my hair done, or to buy a little something for my two girls. Iris too was a sweetie to me and where she tried and failed to get me to glam up for the club, after the Johnny Peach make-over, she gave me a few of her beautiful evening gowns.

CHAPTER TEN

GAEL.

It now seemed perfectly normal to take the next step and become a driver. My husband had finally bought a decent car and had given me half a dozen lessons and I took to the roads like a good 'un. The car was a Hillman Imp, a smart shiny red thing that I loved.

(Gotta tell you that within a few months of passing my test, I had bought myself a car, an ancient black A30 and I called it the 'chugger'. It had creased black leather upholstery and indicators in the form of little yellow plastic arms that came out either side to show which way you were turning. It was not the most stylish statement I had ever made, but I wish I had the thing today!)

After a couple of months I drove everywhere by myself in the Hillman, having assured John I would be very careful and indeed, naughty to admit, I drove for about eighteen months accident free without taking a test. But eventually it was pointed out to me that not only was it illegal, I was foolishly invalidating our insurance in doing this and so I somewhat reluctantly booked a test. I say reluctantly because nothing ever comes easy to me. I had continued to develop the nerves mam always said I didn't have as a child and practised worrying on a daily basis until I was perfect at it.

I worried about the four minute warning and had already mentally if not practically taken the governments advice to take a door off its hinges, cover it with old blankets and old thick coats (where was that bloody grey cat coat of mine now that I needed it?) and once the warning siren started, the government told us to crawl in this 'tent' with my husband and two children and to stay there until the blast had settled. In this way I was led to believe from the leaflet we all got at the time, we could survive a nuclear blast. HONEST! I worried the our house would catch fire, I worried that the Clifton bridge would collapse as we drove over it and had a survival plan worked out wherein I would stuff the baby in my knickers and grab Laura's little hand and jump out before we hit the water! Always best to have a plan no matter how loony! I have to confess worrying came easy to me and it had got so bad that I now had a waiting list for fresh worries! But at this minute, top of the list was my coming driving test.

I was advised to book a few lessons with a school in order to familiarise myself with both the test procedure and the route. This I did, booking a series of lessons with a man called Bernie. On the day of the test I wore a beautiful dress with a low cut neckline, had on sky high stiletto heeled shoes and my Musters face was complete with inch long false eyelashes. I intended to sail through the test and thought the newly acquired albeit false charm of my 'dolly bird' look would not harm my cause! I mean, how could anyone fail me when I had driven so well for the last year and a half anyway?

My teacher met me at the test centre on Musters Road and came with me on a final test run. He would wait until I came back and see how I had done. My tester was an elderly man and I settled down and went confidently through his instructions one by one. To my utter astonishment and chagrin, he failed me. Meeting up with Bernie minutes later, he said he thought I would fail as I was over confident. *He knew I had time to get out of that side road onto a busy main road but the examiner would think I was being careless and would expect me to take a lot longer than a few seconds to pull safely out into the traffic.* He bid me book another test which I did, there and then.

When I got to work at Chambers Bros later, I tearfully told the girls of my failure. June Fox-Smith who had been driving for years gave me some tips and told me what to look for the next time. When I was to do an emergency stop, I would see the examiner look into the rear view mirror. He'd be checking on the traffic behind in order to do this safely and then he'd brace himself before slapping his clipboard to signal me to slam on the brakes. If at any time during the entire test he touched his pad with his pencil it was a failure! The test date soon came round and I was off my head with worry and nerves. This time, I wore a long high necked navy blue dress, clubby heeled shoes, had on very little make-up and wore my ancient white swept away Dame Edna glasses that always reduced my children to helpless laughter whenever I wore them. They were very weak and I actually could see just as well without them but I though they gave me an air of deep concentration. I had left my false eye lashes doing their imitation of a spider on my dressing table! Thus kitted out for my big day I drove like a complete and utter prat.

Not to repeat, which I now do of course, things happen to me. Anyone else would go through the motions with absolutely no trouble but I have a theory in which I see those Greek Gods on high sat in a hall surrounded by elegant marble columns at a marble table which they are idly drumming with bored fingers. Having already given me a lousy hand of cards at birth, which I have wearily at times gritted my teeth and hard played to date, they have no idea what to do with themselves for the day and so look to me to give them their sport as they mess my life up some more. It's truly the only explanation for nothing ever comes easy to me and why should a driving test be any different?

Mind, I also admit it may well be these very same gods that throw me a timely lifeline on odd occasions that permits me to escape a difficult situation. Like the one readers of the 2nd book will testify to when I ruined a new WHITE coat - as in twenty minutes new – and I am sure it was them that gave me the idea if I pulled the damaged part from the inside pocket, I could do a three quarter spin and fool my mother long enough for me to get it fixed, so saving me from her wrath and not for the first time. Phew!

Came the day of the test and I confidently read the number plate on a car parked the required number of yards away. It was to be the only confident move I was to make for the next half hour or so. My tester was a middle aged man with, I decided, mean cruel thin lips. At his behest, I began by easing out of my parked position a little whilst looking carefully over my right shoulder. A bloody great big lorry filled with beer casks was heading for the Musters further down the road and I wisely decided to wait. It took quite awhile as the parked traffic was heavy round the test centre and so narrowed the road making it difficult for such a cumbersome vehicle to pass. As it slowly edged past me and I followed it with my eyes, I realised to my horror I had been steadily if somewhat slowly moving forward all this time and damn near hit the car parked in front of me. Great start. We began to move off and I had to apologise for the sudden sluggishness of the car. Typical I thought, it had been fine until now. In silence the examiner reached out and took the hand brake fully off.

Off we went out into the town. He asked me to turn left and I missed the turning! Not to panic. This had been covered by my driving instructor who had said in the event of this happening, I was to apologise, indicate and take the next left. Now I saw the wisdom of having these extra driving lessons! I duly indicated, pulled on the wheel and turned into a dead end! This event had NOT been covered by my instructor. I saw my tester hit the pad with his pencil....
"I suppose here is as good as anywhere to do your three point turn," he said rather gruffly and unless I was mistaken, a touch sarcastically. I went through the paces slowly and carefully and thought I had executed the manoeuvre pretty well but out of the corner of my eye, I again saw pencil go to pad. He bid me turn left at the next set of lights. I somehow got in the wrong lane and had to indicate my intention to turn right.
"Oh I am so sorry. I shall have to turn right."
"So I see."

Only now did I realise I was at the same junction where I had failed the last test and as I studied the traffic, remembering only too well where I'd gone wrong the last time, I was going to wait a sight longer than the few seconds I'd waited before. I waited so long in fact; I got caught out and was stuck as the lights changed again to red. I had only been behind the wheel but a few minutes and in that time had sweated a river.
"I want you to turn right and in your own good time and at your own convenience, I want you to indicate, safely pull

over into the left hand side of the road, stop the vehicle and switch off the engine,"

I heard that bloody pencil crash down on the clipboard again. I did as he asked and the car died into silence.

"Mrs..........humm" he studied my application form, "..... Blacknell, you are driving like an idiot." He said in a resigned voice. My heart fell into my feet. I was utterly and totally deflated.

"I know and I am sorry, I am just so nervous, I hardly slept last night for worrying."

"Well if you continue to drive like this, I shall have no choice but to fail you. Do you understand?"

My bottom lip began to tremble. I bit hard on it.

"Do you smoke?" he asked.

"Yes I do."

"Then I suggest you have a cigarette and calm down a little before we continue."

I picked up my bag and scrambled about in the bottom, making a mental note to clear it out when I got home. (I did and found Shergar and Lord Lucan!) In an effort to assist me to calm down, he asked was I married, did I have children, where did I live and what did I do for work? I answered him perfunctorily but had calmed down to the point of having no nerves left. Finally finding my fags and lighter, I did as he had suggested and drew deeply on the tobacco, the rush of nicotine having the desired calming effect. There was no way out of this; it was blindingly obvious I had failed yet again. Having stubbed out the half smoked ciggie and at his command, I re-started the engine and went through the rest of the test like an automaton, wanting only for this ordeal to be over and done. Even slamming my brakes on for the emergency stop was simply going through the motions and my hill start was a piece of cake. But that pencil on paper routine continued.

"Pull into the side of the road please." He said brusquely.

I did as he asked, pulled on the handbrake and shut down the engine.

"What is the sequence of traffic lights?"

By now, at this precise moment in time, I didn't know who the hell *I* was let alone what colour traffic lights were. Purple?

"I don't know, I can't think.....Red? Red and amber? ...then green I think, I'm sorry, I just don't know."

In the ensuing silence the tap on his clipboard made more sound than a thousand drums.

"What is the stopping distance at 30 m.p.h?"

I answered as I had driven, like a clockwork toy. A booming silence fell in the car as he hit pencil to the bottom of the pad for the last time.

"Congratulations you have passed."

"**WHAT**?"

"You have passed."

"But..but.."

"Once you got over your nerves I was well satisfied that you can handle this car safely and in all road conditions."

"But, I thought I had blown it. My friend said if I saw you hit your pad with your pencil I had shot it."

"I am not supposed to let you see this."

He held the pad up for me and I saw a neat line of ticks at the side of every one of the manoeuvres I was required by law to make. It was 12.15 Monday 15th July. Memorable enough for me to have put it in my diary! Never have a line of ticks looked so pretty. I kissed him on those previously thought mean cruel lips and would probably have gone further so delighted was I, but luckily he was halfway out of the car!

I went to meet my instructor and gave the game away with my broad grin. Together we tore up my learner plates. That night it was celebrations all round as I legally drove to the Musters for the first time and proudly backed my car straight into the fence breaking my lights and upsetting the neighbours. Now I can honestly tell you that things like that *always* happen to me! Oh I am a prat.

I had got to know quite a few of the regulars in the Musters by now. There was Sheila and Danny; an odd yet strangely perfectly matched couple, he being Scottish and she hailing from Leeds. She was almost a foot taller than him and he was so small and hirsute he looked like a little garden gnome! She had a party trick of picking him up in her arms like a baby. They married eventually and lived with me for quite a while at a couple of my addresses and we were to live with them in Leeds for a while. She is now a widow and still one of my dearest most cherished friends.

Then there were the Pilkington brothers Robin and Gael. Gael was married but had separated from his wife by the time we met. We had nothing in common but we enjoyed each others company and became strong friends. We both had one thing in common, we loved to dance. Most nights there was a party going at the houseboat they owned which was moored under the Trent Bridge. I went to one of these dos but as I don't drink, I don't enjoy watching folks make fools of themselves once they've had a skinful. I just don't understand what pleasure there is in drinking to excess and making yourself and your supposed loved ones suffer badly the next day. Not that I recall Gael being a particularly heavy drinker I hasten to add. But on the odd occasion I went to the Hippo, Parkside or the Pigalle I would happily spend time dancing with him.

One balmy summer night Norman took us all to the Hippo club. My friend Rose had come out for the night and the usual crowd from the Musters also made the trip. For once I had gone in Norman's car because I has wrecked the 'chugger' and the Hillman was in for a service. Gael and I hit the empty dance floor and slid into a rumba. We moved together so well it was as if we'd been taking lessons all our lives but it just came naturally to us.

A group of strange men stood at the far end of the bar and watched us dance for a while and then one of them started to make his way over to us. I smelt trouble and through flashing my eyes, I made Gael aware I did not want to dance with this stranger. He came over and asked if I would dance and quickly Gael excused me and said I was dancing with him.

The man moved back to his friends with a face like thunder. I told Gael to get me a taxi as I was leaving right now. He offered to take me home and we left immediately. He had a pale blue Jaguar at the time and he quickly took me home to Clifton. I begged him not to go back. I had sensed trouble and warned him. But he told me he had promised to take home so many people including Rose and said he thought I was imagining things and he had enough friends down there that would help if he got into trouble he reassured me. I bid him good night and went indoors.

The next day the weather was glorious again as I took Laura to school and Cindy to nursery as usual and stood waiting as I normally did for Rose to join me at the bus stop. As she came towards me, I saw she was covered in tiny bloodied cuts all over her arms, hands, legs and even her face and neck.

124

"What on earth have you done?" I asked shocked.

"You know when to leave don't you? Have you heard from Gael?"

"Why would I hear from Gael?"

"That lad you turned down on the dance floor put a car jack through his windscreen as we were about to go home last night. Gael and I were in the front seat and he copped it full in the face. He is in a right mess."

We jumped on the bus and she gave me the full SP as we travelled along. When we reached Trent Bridge I got off and walked along the towpath to the boat. Climbing aboard I called out his name. There was no reply. I walked along the corridor pushing first one door open and then another. At the fourth attempt I found him. He was laid in bed and to my horror his face was mashed up and he had a small tea plate at the side of his bed which was full of his bloodied teeth. He said he was desperate for a drink but was unable to drink anyway as he could not get the glass over his lips so badly was his mouth smashed.

I returned along the tow path and went to a small café on the bridge and asked them to sell me a bottle of milk and some straws. I took it back and making him as comfortable as I could, held the straw to his mouth so he could drink. He asked me to phone his dentist and make an urgent appointment for him which I did. As I left through painful lips he told me he had fought in both Palestine and Korea without so much as a scratch and he asks me for a dance and loses his front teeth. He was an idiot, I saw it coming and he should have listened. I wonder where he is now....and his brother Robin?

Meanwhile, let me take you back to the Musters.... Thanks to finding my old diary, this next incident can be

125

absolutely dated to the summer of 1968. There was a new Musters hotel guest and he sat in the bar. He looked so odd. He was quite small and thin with greasy sleeked back hair that curled over his collar and though he wore a conventional lounge suit he'd teamed it with rather odd looking orange leather cowboy boots. He just looked out of sync so to speak, certainly not your average business man. His name was Len and we got chatting. He told me of his grandiose plans to bring the first ever Ideal Homes Exhibition to Nottingham later that year.

There would be talent shows, cabaret and he had already booked several popular acts including Sparti a well known midlands sketch artiste who had appeared at the Musters many times. He had also got the local designers to put on fashion shows displaying their work. Clarke's School of Hairdressing also had a stall demonstrating some wonderful wigs and there were to be furniture exhibitions, cookery demonstrations and lots of free samples would be given away. Naturally there would be a beer tent, many small café's and fast food outlets and it would run for a whole ten days. It sounded tremendously exciting. The idea was to set it up in a giant marquee on the Forest ground and he spent a lot of time over the next three weeks selling his ideas to the City Council and sold plots to Nottingham's businessmen.

He had booked Keith Fordyce to compere the talent show and he asked me to do the compering of the fashion show and to sing a song of my own choice before and after the three daily shows. I was asked to model the gowns that were on sale in the show and I also had to wear a different Clarke's wig at every appearance. The money he offered was wonderful. He had booked the Kenny Baker Jazzmen to play in the marquee at the opening ceremony to which the top Nottingham brass, TV and all the press were invited and I too was invited to be there. It was a wonderfully exciting time for me and I lapped it up and why wouldn't I?

For the opening ceremony on Friday the 16th of August, I wore a simple milky grey jersey wool mini skirted suit with shocking pink stilettos, matching bag and finished the outfit off with grey gloves decorated with vivid psychedelic turquoise and pink abstract patterns. The outfit looked really smart. I parked our car alongside the Rollers and Mercedes and mentally wished I had cleaned it before I came. I was not happy going along alone. Even Norman and Iris were away on holiday and the only one I would know there was Len and he'd be too busy selling his product to have any truck with me. Straightening myself up, I nervously headed for the tent which was manned by two tall splendid black men in bright red and gold liveried uniforms with heavily plumed turbans. One asked for my invitation and I gave it to him.

"**MISS JOY JAMES**" he boomed and all eyes turned on me as if I was a somebody. I felt a right prat. There was much pomp and grandeur and a line of uniformed trumpeters blasted the air officially heralding the opening of the show. I hung around like a whatsit at a doodah sipping my glass of champagne and picking at the plates of hors dourves. Then I wandered off to find my dressing room and get ready for the first fashion show....

The exhibition proved to be a huge success and the marquee was crowded with people every hour of the day throughout its entire run. Len must have made a fortune and not a small one either. As the show closed, the designers gave me every dress I had modelled for them and John Clarke gave me a choice of the wigs I had worn. Len thanked me profusely and told me he was taking me out to a special seven course 'thank you' dinner the following week (Friday August 23rd) to see Dave Allen in cabaret at the Parkside. I'd heard he was there and longed to go and see him but the tickets were £25 each, a bloody fortune then and were like gold dust. One of the dresses I had been given at the exhibition was from a local designer called Fanny's. It was in an apple green shantung, was low cut but fitted at the bust and fell away to the floor in an A shape from a central deep pleat. It was without doubt one of the best and classiest dresses I have ever owned. It was quite simply stunning. I decided to wear that.

(I sadly loaned this precious dress to my youngest daughter and the last time I saw it, it was screwed up and covered in oil and rust on her garage floor.)

We had an 'edge of stage' table and sat down to eat. I can still remember every single course, every piece of highly polished silver plated cutlery, every monogrammed dish containing every morsel, every delicious mouthful I ate that night. The meal began with a velvety Vichyssoise soup, which I was surprised to find was served in a bowl sat on crushed ice. I wisely resisted the urge to tell them it was cold!!! Then came a superb pate with a basket of Melba toast, a first for me and I wolfed it down lathered thickly in curls of butter. This was followed by Lobster Thermidor – another first - served in its own shell it was prettily perched on a bed of exotic green salad so I also tasted capsicums for the first time too. Oh man...

The meat course was steak Diane, a new and big hit in those days and was followed by a sweet course an impressive raspberry and Lavender Pavlova. Then came a selection of

My snatched photos

While I was working on 'Nanny'. I couldn't resist taking this shot of Wendy Craig.
For this scene I was in charge of a bus load of wartime kids.
The location is Lincoln in 1981 for BBC TV.

The Consumate Actor Tony Melody on location at Belvoir Castle, Leicestershire in 1980 for 'Little Lord Fauntleroy'.

Likewise the late adorable Elizabeth Spriggs waiting to make her appearance in 'Playing the Field'.

Bagthorpe, Nottingham is the location for 'Sons and Lovers' in 1981 for BBC
TV at 'The Dixies Arms'. I'm somewhere in the crowd at the back.

Left to right: some of the artistes who performed at the Rycote
Centre Variety Show, Derby in May: Jean Couchman, Al Rich,
Joy James, Leo Hudson, John Dennett, Tommy Russell, Ray
Raymond and Sally Treble (organiser).

This is taken from a newspaper cutting

MORE SNATCHED PHOTOS

I took this photo between takes of Brigit Forsyth on the set of 'Inside Out' fot the BBC in 1984.

RIGHT:Kevin Whately on a break from 'Auf Wiedersehen Pet'.

Belvoir Castle in Leicestershire. The set of 'Little Lord Fauntleroy'. I'm useless with a camera as these photos bear witness to.

Alec Guinness being led to the cameras for his scenes at Belvoir Castle in Leicestershire.

Another fine Actor Peter Copley on the set for the same film.

In the good old days before political correctness, my Daughters Zoe and Cindy in fancy dress for a Village party.

on my exit from Equity the acting union, I joined my local parish council. I needed to feel that I was contributing to life in some way and I have found a photo where I am doing just that.
"All the 6's clickety click".

On location for BBC TV's 'Inside out' in 1984.This is a Wedding scene and with me are Daughter Zoe and Annamarie Treble. To the right my dear departed friend Charlie Bartle.

Does it run in the family?

My Daughter Zoe in some of her screen roles

Zoe (RIGHT) with Tim Healy
(Dennis the Foreman) and
Annamarie Treble during filming
of 'Auf Wiedersehen Pet' for
Central TV.

'Auf Wiedersehen Pet'
again and alongside Zoe
is Jimmy Naill (Oz). To
the left is Tim Healy.

Making a pop video.
Zoe is extreme left and
I'm in the car wearing an
original Jane Russell
basque.

Councillor James o'Riordan introduces me for the launch of my second book 'Yo'd Mek a Parson Swear .... Again' at St Ann's Library. Nottingham on the 24th June 2009.

A charity night for 'BLESMA' (British Limbless Ex-servicemen Association).
L to R: Comedian Dave Betton - Malcolm Robinson and me.
The venue. The Manor Club. West Bridgford. Nottingham in 1985.

This was taken during the trip to Blackpool. Doris is on the top row centre wearing a light coloured dress and is aiming an odd look in my direction...

LEFT: An early modelling shot to be used for publicity purposes. This was my Johnny Peach 'makeover'. The dress by Jacques Vert cost all of £1.50 at Nottingham Central Markets.

The late Lynn Perry, star of Coronation Street with me and my Daughter Zoe at the Manor Club, Nottingham in1986.

PHOTO: BBC Radio Nottingham

John Holmes welcomes me at the BBC to talk about my two previous books.

September 2009 I celebrate my 70th birthday and got the rare chance to have all my daughters together at the same time.
LEFT TO RIGHT: Zoe, Laura and Cindy.

This photoshoot was taken in1970 for the Co-op. It was to demonstrate how easy it was to clean Co-op secondary double glazing - NOT!!

PHOTOS:
John Sumpter of Long Eaton.

exotic cheeses and biscuits and finally hand made petite fours. Each course had its own wine too but like I keep repeating I am not a drinker and stuck to water. I had all but done after the Lobster and could not do justice to the rest of the courses, merely picking at them here and there......I could now by the way....if anyone's asking!

Dave Allen was simply superb. He began his show by shaking hands with as many people as he could and clearly knew Len personally. I got to shake his hand too. That man wasn't just good, he was dynamite. My face and sides ached from the laughter. Len took me home in a taxi and said goodnight on my doorstep and I went inside eager to share the night with John. I never saw him again and never ever had as good a meal as that again either....

Jack Denman, my agent, is a nationally known and highly respected business man in these parts and can count many big stars as personal friends. Even though he is now in his 80's he still works from home and indeed I had a residual cheque for £2 odd from him quite recently. For many many years he had a suite of offices in the Elite building on Parliament Street Nottingham from where he ran his Theatrical and TV Casting Agency business. He has booked the very best.

There is a well known story of the time he went to London to recruit some new artistes to the midlands. He stayed down there a couple of days and visited every agent in the phone book. He found that some of the London based acts would not do more than one spot and wanted top dollar for doing it. One agent told him that to book a decent comic he may well have to book two years in advance! He came home virtually empty handed and began to look around the midlands and north gradually building a client base in excess of 600. (Now nearer 1.000 I believe!)

Wanting a good comic for a special Falklands charity show he was putting on at the prestigious Nottingham Concert Hall, he made enquiries of a top London agent. He was offered an 'up and coming' young comic who would do two half hour spots for £25. Having not heard of the man, Jack politely declined. Less than a year later, he phoned that agent again and tried to book this same 'up and coming' comic and was told he had 'up and come' and due to TV commitments was unable to book so far in advance but advised Jack to submit a selection of dates and they would accept a provisional booking subject to his commitments, at a cost of £1000 and he would do a one hour show!!! That man's name was Dave Allen!

CHAPTER ELEVEN

WO'KIN'T MEN'S CLUBS!

One night, as I stood on stage singing at the Musters I noticed a well dressed, not to say tall dapper moustachioed gent avidly watching me. I finished my song, introduced the artiste and moved to the bar to watch the show. The chap stood up, quaffed his drink and came to my side.

"Hello Joy, my name's Val Terry and I'm the local Equity secretary for the East Midlands. I also run the Val Terry Variety Agency. You have a fine singing voice and I like your style. Have you ever thought of working the clubs?"

I shook my head, discounting one unfortunate incident (a few paragraphs further on) as not worth a mention.

"I can find you as much club work as you can handle."

I said I'd think about it, mumbled my thanks as he pressed his card into my hand and left. It ended up along with all the other bits and bobs and the almost compulsory lidless lipstick in the bottom of my handbag. I thought of all the girls who came to the Musters to sing from all over the country and could not imagine me doing that. It had seemed to me to be such hard work. In the fullness of time I was to find out that doing a residency for a long time was twice as hard.

One week we had a girl singer hailing from right here in Nottingham. Her name was Pauline Leybourne. She was neat petite and really sweet. (No pun or rhyme intended!) She had a strong soprano voice which was perfect for her 'songs from the shows' act. She opened with a cheery little number and then said her cheeky hello's to the audience, went into a little of the history of the next song and then proceeded to sing it but to my astonishment as she did so, she slowly peeled off her dress revealing a skimpy little sequinned number that showed her perfect figure off to perfection. I was bemused. She had a lovely singing voice why did she need to do the strip bit?

I was later to find out its nothing to do with showing off one's body and everything to do with competing with bingo, noisy slot machines and the many other entertainments provided by the working men's clubs. It was all to do with grabbing an audience by the scruff of the neck in order to demand and keep their attention. Sat in the audience watching her each night was her manager husband Alan. He was a shrewd business man, had his own entertainment agency and he too proffered his card. This time I put that card safely away in my purse thinking I may one day take him up on it. Pauline and I were to bump into each other professionally from time to time and I often recall some of the conversations we had.

There was another young Nottingham singer coming up at that time too. Her name was Haley and I would have walked over hot coals to hear her sing but as fast as she came to light, she totally disappeared from the musical scene. I saw her out shopping one day and asked why she no longer sang. She told me she had married and her husband had overheard some men in the loo of a club she was working in, pass sexual comment about her. She had never worked since. What a crying shame.

Another lady I would walk the proverbial hot coals to hear sing was a very well known songstress named Jill Ball who sang regularly with the Harry Brown set. She was a 'singers' singer with a love of jazz and a phraseology second to none. I loved her work. A few years ago, I came across Harry in the Five Ways pub. He was sat gentling the piano into giving out some beautiful melodies to an appreciative audience. Spotting me, he called me to his side and asked me to sing. I was flattered he even knew of me and obliged. I was with a male friend at that time and he had no idea I could sing. I sang 'Summertime' to Harry's accompaniment and we got an astonishing round of applause, not least from my escort. Towards the end of the evening I was asked to sing another and the two of us did justice to that old classic Little Boy if Daddy Goes Away (ask yer great gran!). My escort was amazed and said he had not only never heard that song before but had never seen anyone bring a rowdy audience to utter silence and at eleven o clock at night too. Getting a reaction like that is the icing on the cake. That night Harry begged me to start up a duo with him but I had long since been out of that side of the business and felt no need to begin again. I have always bitterly regretted that rash decision.

I had thought of doing club work some years prior and had approached the Jimmy Haynes agency. He was a tall tubby man with a nasally way of talking and had an office at that time, on Aspley Lane. I made an appointment and went along to see him. There was another man in his office that afternoon, one Johnny Johnstone an exceedingly well known musician of his day. I had prepared myself to sing a lovely song and after the introductions, waited to be asked to show him my vocal chords, but he surprised me by saying "Show us your legs!"

"What?"

"Yer legs girl, show us yer legs!"

What the flock had my legs got to do with my singing I wondered as they both watched me hitch my skirt up to my knees!

"Get them bloody skirts up and show us yer legs girl."

I took them as far as shame would permit me to, not 'shame' as in shame more as in being a-shamed I *had* such awful thick legs and those even thicker ankles that mam had drummed into me I had! He glanced down over his desk at my display and I think he agreed with mam and didn't request I go any higher. He was looking for those well known Stork legs, the ones that spread easy! Mine may well have never stopped a 'pig in an entry' as mam would have it, but they weren't spread easy either! Only now as my skirts dropped did he ask me to sing. I sang a few bars of something or other and got rewarded with the raising of his eyebrow.

On the strength of that 'audition' he booked me to sing on a charity show he was organising at the YMCA in town. He asked what did I sing and I gave him a few titles. He asked Johnny to sort me out a spot to do on that night. Johnny Johnstone transposed about five or six songs for me and I have never ever seen such beautifully written 'dots' in my life, they were works of art. I still have them albeit a bit dog eared after all these years of use.

Come the night of the show, I turned up and was amazed at just how many people were to perform. Far from being thrilled to have been chosen to work on it, I was once again bloody terrified. There were two dressing rooms side by side, male and female. I opened the door and went in. The room was empty but someone was already ensconced in there by the time I arrived. Beautiful glittering stage dresses hung one on top of another and several pairs of gold and silver shoes were lined up beneath them. I looked down at my simple unglamorous C&A 9s/11d cotton day dress. It was all I had and I could have wept. The door opened slowly and a head appeared round it. The 'head' was a ventriloquist's dummy!

"Hello!" 'It' said,

"Did you know;
a man's not old when his hair turns grey?
nor is he old when his teeth decay
he's only old when he goes to sleep
and dreams of appointments he can't keep!"

The head was followed by a real head, a laughing dark haired real 'ladies man's' head, the head of the exceedingly good looking and talented well known ventriloquist Neville King. We were to go on to work together on many many occasions but meanwhile I had a stage act to worry about. (*Neville King died in August 2009 aged 81.*)

I was joined by my fellow dressing room colleague. She was a glamorous, dark haired lass of about my age and she asked where my clothes were and I told her this was it, smoothing my ten bob special over my tummy as though that would enhance it in some way. She reached up to the hook and rifled through those lovely dresses and handed me one. "Here, wear this, I am sure it will fit you and suit you too." She said kindly. Sad to say, I can no longer recall this lady's name but it was a wonderful gesture and I still thank her for it. (I actually wrote to the Nottingham Evening Post and told them of this incident and they printed it.)

But if wearing the dress was meant to relieve the pressure I was under, it failed and I did a re-run of my Opportunity Knocks appearance, running like Linford Christie off the stage as the last note died! (ME? Work the clubs? Gerrauntonit!) I never heard from Jimmy again until some years later when I had become well established in the business. By this time, I knew OF him and knew him to be a crafty old bugger that would make a small fortune out of you if you were not careful.

"Joy...Jimmy here..." those nasal tones never altered no matter his age, "..got a little gig will suit you well...Boot and Shoe Leicester... £10 no pick up."

A 'no pick up' meant that you did not get paid by the club; they instead paid your fee to the booking agent who in turn paid you. It had begun as a way of agents getting money owed them by artistes. Often this could run into several hundreds of pounds and it had seemed like a good idea at the time but some agents then used it as a way of doubling their commission fee's, Jimmy was a prime example!

"Oh ay, an' what yo' gerrin' forrit then eh?" I asked him. "Never yo' mind what ah'm gerrin forrit, it's a tenner to yo' an' ah'sll want ten per cent commission on that bogger annall...." and he was not joking. Oh he was a crafty *rich* old sod. But I liked and respected him, working for and with him many times throughout more years than I care to remember. He never asked to see my legs again! Wise man.

It was on a return visit to the Musters by Pauline Leybourne and her husband Alan Bagguely that finally got me on the club circuit proper. He asked what I was earning at the moment doing a week at this place. I told him. He rolled his eyes up and said he could pay me double that for one twenty minute spot midweek at the Mucky Duck (Grey

Goose Gedling) and triple that for a job at the weekend. Only first I had to get ready. 'Getting ready' meant having an expensive phone put in, sorting out transport and being ready to go at the drop of a hat. I had the phone put in, (Nottingham 241549 I would trill...!) I had no problem with transport. However, those who know me will by now be smiling, knowing only too well that having transport is one thing, getting there with absolutely no sense of direction whatsoever, is quite another! I could write a whole book about getting lost... Here's a classic:

A friend of mine was going into hospital for a cosmetic face lift. She put on a brave front but I knew she was terrified and begged me to go and see her after she had the operation. One bright spring day I set off and to my astonishment found myself in the Victoria Centre car park! What the dickey thump was I doing here? Oh well, being's as I was here now.., I might as well get some flowers and a treat for her. I picked up a bouquet and a box of as yet out of season and therefore expensive strawberries. Back in my car, I realised I had no idea where I was going. She was in the Park Hospital and I don't think I had ever been there and yet.... I had a vague idea and sitting in my car in the gloomy underground car park, I mentally came back from whence I thought it to be. It was all the way up the Mansfield road, left at the roundabout and first right at the traffic lights! Got it! I duly and confidently set off and arrived at the right place. Who said I was an idiot where directions were concerned? I walked into that building ten feet tall toting my goodies. I smiled at the receptionist and asked to see Mrs X. She tapped the name into her computer. Err, how am I spelling that? I

carefully spelt her surname and watched as she scoured the
screen.
"Can you come back tomorrow after 10 o'clock please?"
Alarm spread through me,
"Why, has something gone wrong, is she ill?"
"No, that's when she's booked in!"
I gave the receptionist a bunch of flowers and a box of out of
season strawberries as I left with my tail between my legs!

The first booking I received from Alan Bagguely over my nice new green telephone was for the aforementioned Grey Goose. It was as he had said, a mid week booking and it paid the unheard of sum of £8. This was quickly followed by a job in Sheffield where I was to discover just how hard club work can be. There's a saying in the business that if you are a ten quid artiste in your home town, the fact that you have had to travel several hundred miles in one night does not make you a twenty quid act. The fee, despite all that travel was £6.

Let me try and put into perspective what club life is like; the clubs fill early with all ages bagging their favourite seats, their ages ranging from babes in prams through to toddlers, teenagers and octogenarians. It's not unknown for harassed parents to dump their kids in their local club, load them up with pop and crisps and then leave them as they go off to another more sedate club, whilst their kids run riot. As 'act f'ot neet' you have to be careful where you sit as you'll soon be told 'yo munt sit there serreh that's Nobby's seat' or, 'don't sit there lass, that's where thi' sell't bingo books.' Soon after arriving you are seen by the club concert secretary who will tell you what is required of you.

"Three twenty minutes spots lass, ten past eight, ten past nine and half past ten. Wi' got good backin' 'ere, our lads are the

best. Thi'll not be many in fo't last spot mind as thi' all go 'ome once the bingo jackpots been played." Hmmmm.
As I came off after the first spot, I remarked to the chairman that they don't go a bundle on applause do they?
"Nobody gives these lads a round of applause when they come up from t'pit duthi'?"

How do you get a room full of women to mumble 'Aw shit!' in unison? Shout BINGO when they are all waiting for one number! I know, I did it in Stoke on Trent one Christmas eve and won the jackpot of £98, a not inconsiderable amount back then. The club secretary was so angry as I picked up my winnings, he told me I would never work that place again and I never did! Ditto on another club, I worked there one night in Scunthorpe and played the slot machine. I had put in a couple of quid and dropped the jackpot of £100. Along raced a committee member who told me I could not have that money as it was for members only. I scooped it all up and threw it into my handbag and sweetly told him he had watched me put the money in and there should have been a notice barring non club members from playing. That money went home with me and I did work that place again more than once and there was still no notice on the machine but I gave it a miss from then on anyway.

But back to my first club date in Sheffield; my first husband drove me and took about three hours to get us there. He complained bitterly having no concept of the distance one could be expected to travel in one night (I expected him to know better, don't forget he was a transport manager for a large company!) and he advised me to give it up as a job not worth doing. From then on, I did it myself driving there and

139

back, sometimes with a friend for company and sometimes alone. Steadily painfully and sometimes comically I began to learn my craft. I noticed that most artistes had their own P.A gear (public address system) and got a much nicer sound than I did as I merely relied on the clubs own bingo microphone that sounded as if I was singing under water or through a cushion! I bought a small system second hand. It was very heavy but just about manageable by me or by any punter who just happened to be daft enough to stop and offer to help. The sound though was beautiful.

Where the musicians were concerned I had no choice but to use the clubs own. It was odd, all the clubs I worked had the 'best musicians in the country' and sometimes they *were* pretty good. I could very quickly pick up on the musician's reaction to my 'dots'. If he – and it was mainly a 'he' – casually whipped through them in seconds with a 'yeah..yeah...yeah...', despite being assured by the clubs concert secretary 'he' was the best keyboard player in town - I knew I was in trouble. Conversely the 'he' that said 'just hum this intro for me pet, yes, I think its ok, but if I falter, just keep going,' was a pretty safe bet. Any vocalist will tell you its musicians like this that make a song you have sung a thousand times before, stand out like a beacon. But when the backing is bad, and in some cases it was appallingly bad, I just had to 'keep going' reminding myself that every act had the same backing and the audience would judge me on my entertainment value.

And here, let me tell you something that might surprise you, you can sing a song that one thousand times but the next time you can forget the words! Your mind goes a complete blank and out comes gibberish until the real words come back and you can continue. Oh and beware when learning words that you don't fall into the trap of learning them wrongly! Let me explain; whilst working at the Commodore we had to be bang up to date with the top twenty whether we liked the songs or not and in the hit of the day 'Hey Look Me Over....lend me your ear.....(and it was a song I **hated**!)', it ends, 'I'm a little bit short of the elbow room so let me get me some...' and for some inexplicable reason it came out of my mouth as 'I'm a little bit short in the afterbirth, so let me get me some!' Ever after that the lads would hang on my words, willing me to sing it wrong! And in 1960 I was required to learn another lovely song Gigi from the show of the same name. There is a line in it that says '...was I out yonder somewhere winking at a star'. It came out of my mouth as 'was I out wander somewhere yinking at a star!' Once I had sung it that way, it was very hard to correct.

One's fellow artistes can also be summed up pretty quickly as soon as they enter a dressing room. They have only to open their mouths or not as the case may be. I recall one Leslie Lewis a quite simple looking man - and no I don't mean daft, I mean simple as in uncomplicated - he instantly gave me the feeling that I could have trusted him with my life, the sort of man who would have no trouble selling you a life insurance policy. He came into the shared dressing room and immediately passed comment on the coldness of the night, asked did I want a drink, sorted out the times he was to go on chatted amiably about this and that without once mentioning his act and melted into the crowded club until it was time for his spot. He wasn't at all good, he was sensational.

And if there is the quiet little man who can get an audience eating out of his hand, there is also the reverse too; the man who bustles through the door and tells you how he slaughtered them last night, how they pleaded with him to come back soon for double the fee, how he was in line to get his own TV show.....it would not be a good night and I have seen such acts have the curtain pulled across their noses within seconds. When a comic is good he is usually very good but when he is bad ohhhh, forget it. Fortunately there are far more good ones than there are bad. The bad ones don't seem to stay around too long.

There were nights when everything went right and those times were so precious, so utterly rewarding I can never forget them and the mere thought of them still brings a tear to my eye. The introduction format rarely alters, it's almost as though the concert secretaries work from a word perfect but unwritten script. Standing in the wings waiting for your cue, he is building up his introduction to the inevitable crescendo;

".......and so give a **** working men's club welcome and put your hands together as I bring onstage Miss *Joy JAMES....*" A loud blast of organ/piano music was my intro to my first song and would precede my run onto the stage. I'd pick up the mike and sing...

"HELLO, young lovers whoever you are...." now the adrenaline would kick in and I was up and at 'em. It was always the first few notes the backing played that signalled what I would sing that night. On occasion, few and far between I might add, I would turn to the musicians as I sang with my eyebrows raised in sheer delight and as the first song died away, I'd tell them to throw the 'dots' on the floor and we would have a blast doing all the old classics and doing them justice. I have had some truly wonderful nights like that and the bonus was, I not only got paid but got my name put up on the foyer notice board in coloured chalks on a much heralded return visit.

And that's another thing; I once went to a club and found when I got there, they'd advertised on their foyer board in white chalk the act for that night as being a male singer by the name of George Hames. (Joy James?) When they realised they had mis-heard my name over the phone, the concert secretary told me huffily 'We don't book women 'ere, they don't go down very well!' (Gee thanks a bunch!) I did a bomb and went back many times. Occasionally I got to go to clubs that really **did** have some of the very best backing in the country let alone the county and oh what a joy they were. But with the unknown night stretching before me, I would stand waiting in the wings or behind the tabs and I'd question what the hell I was doing here. I hated this I would tell myself and I'd much sooner be at home ironing, scrubbing the kitchen floor or watching something ANYTHING on the telly than stood here.

I was once booked to do the Payne's Label social club in Peterborough. I vividly recall that night with warmth and pleasure. It was a long room packed to capacity and with quite a few children in the audience, not usually a good sign but these kids were unusually well behaved and I was told why. The reason being; any child who did not behave was ousted by the committee along with their parents and were barred for a certain length of time from all the firms activities and there were many it appeared. It worked.

The high professional stage was to the left as we came through the door and we turned right and walked halfway down the room where a glass 'office' had been erected as a committee room. This was to be our dressing room for the night. Wonder of wonders, it had a coloured TV and I had never seen one to watch for any length of time. A few minutes later, who should walk in but Leslie Lewis and we greeted each other warmly.

I went on stage and did my first spot followed by Leslie. Instead of sitting in the concert room as I usually did, I watched the TV but I heard the thunderous applause as he ended his hour long spot. Unable to drive and unwilling to learn, he went everywhere by public transport and so as soon as he was done, he took his leave of us in his long fawn overcoat trilby hat and clutching his small brown suitcase. As the night wore on the usual bingo took over but the TV had now got me hooked and I stayed put glued to this box.

When I was called on for my last spot it was showing that surreal film about Dennis Weaver being dogged by a mysterious truck and I was reluctant to leave but I answered the call and had a really exceptionally good reaction from that audience with the help of the 'hum a bit' backing, forty five minutes later I finally said my good nights. I then raced back to catch the last ten minutes of that tense thriller. As I watched I packed. The credits rolled and I picked up my gear, left the 'office' and began the long walk down the room. To my surprise, not a man woman or child had gone. The room was still packed to the gills. As I walked a man stood up and applauded me, followed by another and another, until the whole room was up on their feet rapturously applauding. By the time I got to my car, I was weeping copiously and *then* I knew exactly why I did it!

(It was on the back of that night that we got our first coloured TV set!)

144

Funnily enough that aforementioned club in Scunthorpe where I dropped the jackpot turned out to be one of those 'special' places. I remember it was summertime and the club was lit by daylight for a change. I did all the lovely old Irving Berlin and Cole Porter numbers and the audience began to shout out songs they wanted me to do. I sang for the first time ever, Shirley Basseys Gold Finger and I didn't do a half bad job on it either to my surprise. Towards the end of the last spot, a man walked down the centre of the long room and stood in front of the very high stage at my feet. I leaned down to him and he asked me to sing Moonlight in Vermont. I knew it but had never actually sung it before in my life. But by now, I would have trusted those musicians with my life and asked them if they could sort a key out for me and I gave it a go.

The way those lads played, coupled with the way I sang bought the house down. As I packed up to go home, the man again took the long walk down the emptying room to the stage and asked me for a card and a photograph. He thought I would do well at such and such a place down the road. This is said in every club every night but I happily gave him my card and signed a photo to him. It was a lovely return journey home that night as I basked in their applause and I wished a thousand times every night could be this good. The next day there was a knock at the door and I was handed a HUGE bouquet of flowers....no it was bigger than that. A card attached said;

'Had I known you were going to give us such a nice night, I would have arranged for these to be given you on stage last night'.

They were from Mr Moonlight in Vermont!

Another club I loved was the Alexander Club in Grimsby. It had a large stage with dressing rooms either side, one for males and one for females and very sensibly and considerately attached to each one was a loo but access was via the stage only so unless you got off pretty sharpish after your spot, you were trapped in your dressing room as the next act got underway almost immediately. It was run by a lovely flamboyant almost foppish character that waited on his artistes hand and foot. He was nothing if not absolutely professional in every way. But he warned every artiste as they set foot in the place that if they were not totally finished on stage, including the so called 'false tabs' by 10pm, he would pull the plug on them as bingo took over from then till closing time. He was not joking. 10pm? We could be home before midnight! Wow.

I had two spots and the comic took the centre one. The musicians were the 'just hum this bit' breed of backing and I opened up the show and began to sing. They were a wonderfully appreciative audience and I had their total attention from the off. I closed my first spot with a much loved ballad enhanced by the superb backing and left the stage to thunderous applause. Wow again.

The second spot was no different and with one eye on the clock, again bought the house down. As the club readied itself for the bingo, I hastily packed up my stuff and headed for the door. All the way down the room folks stopped me, told me what a lovely voice I have, what a lovely show I had put on, shook my hand and asked would I come again? By the time I got to the top of the room and out of the door into the foyer, I was in serious danger of getting a big head. Tucked into a corner, sat at a small round table, a pint of stout within easy reach was a little, very old lady.

146

"Yer sounded like a bloody scalded cat ter me."
My head quickly deflated and I smiled as I went into the night, telling myself "yo' can't win 'em all girl."

On the way up to that club that first night, we had passed a seemingly ultra smart cabaret venue that screamed a name I would have walked those hot coals for; MARTI CAINE. We nosed the car into the car park. It was members only but explaining we had just been to the Alexander club working, they let us in and we had dinner and watched her work. She put on a superb show although I was shocked at some of her racy humour. But when she began to sing I Miss the Hungry Years, I loved her and was an even bigger fan. From that night on I took an interest in her and all she did, all that she achieved. It was an awful loss when she died so young and so tragically.

I did play that Grimsby club several more times but one night was totally memorable for a different reason. By now, I knew the routine inside out, knew the kick off to be 8pm sharp and having had the 'dots' read through, readied myself in the dressing room. I was opening in my glamorous long, split to the thigh black dress. It was bra topped with narrow rhinestone encrusted shoulder straps. I was still (even unto this day!) a martyr to nerves and just had to have a quick wee before I was ready to go on. I don't know if the fact that it was a girl only dressing room was a help or not that night but since I knew no-one else would come in, I left the loo door open and relieved myself. There was a simultaneous bang, whoosh and black out but for the massive wall of flame that enveloped the whole electricity switchboard immediately on the wall in front of me. The whole electrical system had exploded and I was trapped in the loo. Without even thinking, I kicked my panties off my ankles, lifted the dress up and over my head and ran out onto a thankfully blackened stage! Phew!

Artistes are much in demand at Christmas for private functions and annual staff dinners. There is a factory in Melton Mowbray that makes Stilton cheese. It was their Christmas dinner dance and I was only one of the artistes for the night. I stood at the bar sipping my usual orange or grapefruit juice and was approached by their (as it turned out) M.D. All along the bar were huge truckles of Stilton cheeses with varying amounts missing. He took a cheese knife, cut a large chunk out and popped it blissfully into his mouth. I shuddered, a motion not lost on him and he asked didn't I like the cheese? I told him honestly that I didn't like it as my dad had always told us when he was a boy he went round the district selling the stuff and it was riddled with maggots. But had I ever actually tasted it he asked? Well no, I readily admitted and I wasn't about to try.

He then pointed out that it was a bit harsh of me to shudder at the very product that was going to pay my wages that night. He was determined before the night was out I would taste it and putting the knife into the centre of the truckle bought out a mere smidgen and held it out to my mouth. The smell was nauseating. Even though he was laughing he was not about to give up and so I took the proffered pea sized bit and made to swallow it as fast as I could but then got the taste of it. To his and my own great joy I LOVED it and took the remainder of one of those truckles home.

I had by now if anything, too much work on and really had no reason to still work flogging myself to death as a sewing machinist and so, just before Christmas I gave my day job up. The relief of not having to dash about any more was wonderful. I could leisurely take my fast growing children to and from school, do my house work and still have oceans of time to do whatever I wanted for myself before picking the kids up again and maybe taking them on the park or to the cinema for some special together time.

A lot of artistes used to go on ten day runs. This meant they took a package that could see them do at least ten and up to a dozen different clubs on this one run. I was asked to do it many times but though I may be a nut at maths, the figures just didn't add up to me. I reckoned by the time I had taken off the agents 10 percent plus, ten days digs, ten days petrol, ten days babysitting and ten days incidental expenses, what remained wasn't worth leaving my kids for. But then nothing was worth leaving my kids for. The most I ever left them was one week when I went to Bristol and one weekend when I went to Bielefeld in Germany about 1976.

It was a package show with organist Johnny Penny, comedian Joey Simca, magician Shahid Malik and me. I travelled with Johnny in his dinky white van that attracted a lot of continental attention and we shared the expenses of the journey. It had been arranged that we'd meet up with our host Tony Watson and the others at the Beilefeld base itself. We took a night ferry crossing and because it was long, I had used up a sizeable portion of my fee to book an overnight cabin thinking to arrive nice and fresh the next morning. What a waste of money that was. The sea was rough and the boat tossed incessantly. Overhead in the room above the cabin something had fallen and it rolled heavily with the wake of the ship, all the way that way and all the way back all through the night.

If the ferry trip had been long, the journey to Beilefeld was an even longer drive down. I could have slept like a log on a clothes line by now but Johnny begged me to stay awake to keep him from falling asleep. When we finally arrived, we were more than a bit worried when we saw the sandbags stacked ten feet high around the base perimeter. It seems the IRA had just bombed it. Obviously I must have seen and heard of this through the media but as usual didn't connect it with the Beilefeld I was going to and it wasn't in the best interests of the agent to tell me either!

No sooner had we freshened up than it was time to do the opening show and that was right there in the Bielefeld base. Being the last to arrive, there was barely enough time to grab a quick introduction. After we'd got hastily acquainted, we set up our gear, arranged the running order and managed to have a quick rehearsal. We were shattered from the long journey but put on our bright and bushy tailed front and slipped into professional mode.

Although we had only just met, we all worked well together and after doing the first show which took the audience by storm, we went our separate ways, dog tired. The lads were staying at the base but I was lodging at Tony's house and I literally fell into my bed. His wife woke me up the next morning and suggested if I wanted to see the town, we should go like now before they closed as it was the once monthly weekend when all the shops closed early for a long rest. After a hurried breakfast Tony drove me to meet the others and took us all into the centre which was quite close to the base and left us to it. We wandered about for a while taking in the sights and shopping in the mall where I bought the kids a gift each as I was wont to do and then the shops started to close.

We came out of the mall and began a long lazy walk back. Our route took us over a major road and though the lights were against us, we simply skipped over dodging the traffic without recourse to the official crossing. Drivers pipped and folks shouted at us and gesticulated angrily as we jay walked. I gathered they took their road safety a lot more seriously than we did at home. A couple of minutes later we had gone no further than a few hundred yards when a green police car pulled into the kerb and as it slowly stopped an officer jumped out, went down on one knee and aimed a short rifle at us.

"You are under arrest. Please do not move." he called.

The other officer got out and came over to us. He looked directly at me and asked me my name. I told him. He asked Johnny his and he just as politely replied. The officer seemed not at all interested in the others, just Johnny and me.

He asked for our passports but they were back in the base and he told us we should carry them with us at all times whilst we were in Germany. He now turned to the others and asked what we were doing in Germany and collectively we told him we were entertainers working the British bases hereabouts. Meanwhile the one with the gun had slipped back into the car and was relaying all the info we were giving his companion into a mouthpiece. Finally he asked us our contact and we told him it was Sergeant Tony Watson and after he had checked the information we had given him and had it verified, they let us go. We giggled our way back to the base camp thinking what a story we had to tell when we got home to England. Shahid said it made a change to watch white people be arrested!

Back at the base, we found out what all the fuss had been over. It was nothing to do with the jay walking we had supposed it to be, but it seems they were looking for a man and a woman in connection with the recent Beilefeld base

151

bombing and we were ringers for the wanted Irish duo. Tony showed us the two pencilled sketches of the wanted people and it was uncanny how like them we two were; the woman with long blonde hair and my shaped face and the only difference with Johnny was the length of his hair. The rest of the frantically busy weekend went without further incident.

On the Monday morning we began our long homeward journey. Now bearing in mind my tendency not to see things and be totally unobservant; on the way down I *had* taken note of a couple of football stadiums on my left hand side, memorising their names to tell my husband when I got back. As a football fan, I knew he'd be interested. After the long weekend, the return to work traffic heading out of the major towns on the autobahn was really heavy and we began to realise we were going to have to put our foot down if we were to make that ferry crossing in time. Then I saw on my left the football stadium again.

"We are going the wrong way." I told Johnny.

"No, we're not."

"Yes we are, we passed this stadium on the way down and its still on my left and it should surely be on my right!"

He trusted me and putting his foot down to the floor headed straight on, turned at the next giant intersection and made good the thirty or so miles we were adrift. We made that crossing by the skin of our teeth....

CHAPTER TWELVE

RAMPTON

The work I received from Alan was as varied as you could *not* probably imagine. It could be the elegant Friary in Derby one night or the swish Lakeside Cabaret club in Lincolnshire the next. RAF Scampton, Newton and other air or army bases were regulars as was the Combustible (fireman's) Club in Derbyshire or the Rampton Hospital Prison. Being at home all day meant I was now free to go and do the afternoon Rampton shows he put on for the inmates and over the years there were many. I looked forward to doing these shows but my first visit was a real eye opener.

We were met at the gates by uniformed officers who had huge heavy jingling bunches of keys hanging from a thick chain attached to the massively thick leather belt around their waists. He took us into the main building which had an odd school like scent, a mixture of urine, floor polish and disinfectant. We followed behind him like proverbial sheep as he took us down what seemed to be miles of highly polished corridors with heavy multi locked doors every few yards; we arrived at the concert hall which was again behind impenetrable locked doors. This led into a small dressing room with a steep staircase up to the stage. As soon as we were safely inside this dressing room, the officer took his leave noisily locking the door behind him. That door remained locked until after the show when the staff gave us a sumptuous afternoon tea. The actual concert hall was huge. There were banks of chairs to the left and right with a wide expanse of empty highly polished oak flooring centred between the two.

Alan used to put on a complete show and that meant taking along a pianist. On a lot of those shows, Cyril Mayes was the man. He knew my stuff inside out and I could totally trust him. Before the show we all had to have stage wear and props vetted! A parson came in and spoke with the comedy act. They did a funny thing in which one of them walks onto the stage carrying a bowl of swimming gold fish. He takes one of the wriggling little fish and eats it with relish, smacking his lips and licking his fingers one by one. They were in fact strips of carrot!

"Oh no no no... You cannot do that, it may upset the inmates and that would never do."

Another part of their show involved a bucket of water which they flicked at each other and would keep harking at and threatening to throw over the audience, when the throw time comes, it's just a switched bucket full of confetti. That too was stopped. Then they did a rendition of My Boy Lollipop and that ended with them throwing lollipops into the crowd. OH NO NO NO! By the time he had done, half their act had been censored!

Now he turned his attention to me and looked through my gowns. He carefully examined my long black thigh high split dress.

"Tut...oh no, that won't do!"

Next he looked at my salmon pink mini dress with the high neck.

"Ohhh tut, tut, not at *all* suitable."

"What on earth is wrong with them?" I asked in bewilderment.

"What you have to remember is the majority of male offenders in here are sexual offenders. You must wear nothing suggestive."

I did the first show in my long black dress with the side split pinned together and with a football scarf slotted through the straps to cover up my ample bosom. (Since these shows took place once a month and I was to do quite a few of them, I made a wardrobe of inoffensive clothes to wear there and no where else.)

On my first opening show the music swelled and I raced out on stage to the most tumultuous round of applause. I stopped dead and turned to look behind me as I was sure Tom Jones at the very least had just walked on stage after me. My heart was thumping. I didn't know how to treat them. Were they normal or were they – I hesitate to say – not quite all there? I began to sing. After a few bars I settled down some but still looked nervously around at the audience. The men were on my left and the other side were women and these were, sad to say, mainly Downs Syndrome patients. On the front row nearest the vacant centre aisle was a man who was I should think, in his early thirties. He seemed to have a jaded 'seen it all, done it all before' demeanour and with his head resting on his hands and his elbows in turn rested on his knees, he looked bored stiff. I got the impression he had seen too many of these shows and I was just about certain he was either a trustee or even one of the staff. He kept looking down in what I thought to be boredom...until I saw what he was looking at. Let's just say a certain part of his anatomy had escaped! Phew, from then on I could not look anywhere else!

Club dressing rooms are anything from the beer cellar, with innumerable crates stacked one on top of another to provide one with a flat surface to position one's make-up mirror and also provide enough clearance for my, by now, wardrobe of glamorous stage gowns; or it could be someone's living room in the back of a small social club or pub, to a full scale 'worthy of the London Palladium' dressing room with ample space and oceans of mirrors surrounded by dozens of light bulbs most of which worked and anything in between. They vary enormously in size and even cleanliness and some still bore the stale scent of the strip show held the night before, whilst others can smell like a gent's toilet and that's because they are adjacent to the men's toilets or on one occasion *were* a man's toilet! Honest!

Their decorations are to be admired too; almost every artiste who has ever appeared at any club proudly puts his or her photo on the wall but then runs the risk of finding it defaced when next he or she goes back to the club. One such photo bore the legend; '***** ***** from the Himalayas!' under which someone had scrawled '*Like Yak Shit!*' Women would find their previously glamorous photos adorned with horns, their dentistry with blacked out teeth. They'd find additional facial hair in the style of a Groucho moustache and goatee beard and in Stoke on Trent I recall a neat little legend over a tiny washbasin that read; 'Lita Roza has pissed in this sink!' and she had signed it too.

Some, like Lincoln city football club, have ground floor dressing rooms with windows whose skimpy and flimsy curtains leave a lot to be desired and what made me aware one night that I was being watched as I got into my stage dress? I don't know, but I turned like lightning and threw back those useless curtains and saw an elderly man in a trilby hat loping away fast across an empty yard.

Another dressing room I recall was at the Newton air base. Inside the large clean and airy room was a huge metal cabinet full of all sorts of expensive electrical goods like radio's, toasters, irons, cassette tape recorders, and shavers and similar. I passed comment to the young airman who took me in.

"What on earth is all that?" I asked.

"Oh its prizes for raffles and competitions the social club runs."

"Is this the usual dressing room all artistes use?"

"Oh yes, we only ever use this room."

"What and you leave the door unlocked when artistes visit?"

"Yes, we have to, the key's gone missing. Why do you ask?" he said.

"I'd take a bet that some of those boxes are empty." I replied Instantly he paled visibly and pulled one out anxious to prove me wrong. It was empty, as was the next and the next and the.....

Moral; never leave anything of value in a dressing room.

By now, I had picked up quite a bit of comedy patter along the way and was able to entertain between songs too. I do not ever think of myself as being a comedienne, just someone with a line of amusing audience interaction between songs. Alan now trusted me enough to put me with some really big artistes and I would think one of the biggest in those halcyon days was Dick Emery. He was on at the Regency Rooms in Ilkeston. It was for an expensive dinner/dance. I opened the show in a black velvet mini skirted low cut dress. I did a good spot setting the audience up nicely for Dickie, the star of the show.

When he had finished he came into my dressing room and asked me why I was wasting my time doing shows like this when I had all it took to be mainstream. He offered to manage me and put me on a salary of £2.000 for a ten day run. It was a HUGE amount of money then (our first near new house - this one - a four bedded detached, had cost £4,950!) He told me it would be hard work and that mostly I would do one and sometimes two or even three shows a day. He would make sure I had the best laid on for me and my only responsibility would be to get myself there on time and to do a good show.

I pointed out that I had a family of small children and how could I leave them for so long? He gave me his card, told me that's what women do in this business if they want the success, told me to think about it and to give him a ring the next day. If his wife (I seem to recall him saying her name was Josephine) answered I was to tell her who I was and give her my answer and if it was yes, he would be in touch. It didn't take me long to come to a decision and I did call the next day and spoke to a female whom I took to be his wife and turned him down. I then destroyed his phone number so as not to be tempted again. My kids came first.

The clubs themselves can be great levellers. The very next day after the Dick Emery show, I was at the Royal Naval Club in Nuneaton. It was an odd little place in those days, and had been built I seem to remember by knocking two semi detached houses into one. It was a lazy summer afternoon and as I arrived I was greeted by a parson in full white ceremonial garb. He explained that it was the nth anniversary of the sinking of the 'something or other' ship during the last war. He would make a speech and then he would introduce me. Fine. I quickly and quietly set up my gear in this almost churchlike reverence. In subdued terms he began to talk about the lost souls on that fateful ship and he named them one by one. The stiff upper lip began to crumble as the audience remembered the young lost lads. He talked to the gathered 'comrades' about Johnny, George and Arthur, Kenneth and William 'and let's not forget comrades, little Billy and Fred', of their great sacrifice, of their loss still so very keenly missed despite all these years. And without further ado, he then announced;

"And as we remember comrades, I would ask you to please put your hands together and welcome Miss Joy James."

Two people clapped, not the thunderous round of applause I had expected. I was gob smacked. Half the audience were in floods of tears and the other half were in no mood for light entertainment. I sang my first 'throw away' song and I threw it away! Then dedicated every one I sang after that to our poor lost comrades, naming them one by one! What the hell else could I have done? I wondered what Dick Emery would have made of THAT show?

Another type of show I must cover is the strip shows. I was never truly comfortable doing these things and the odd thing was the very guys who had booked some of the naughtiest women on the circuit *and joined in with them in some very dubious acts*, at the end of the performance would come to me and tell me how much they respected me and whatever I did I was *not* to take my clothes off. You mean I needed telling? I had already turned down the chance to be the only singing stripper on the circuit. No matter how well it was paid and it was paid double what I was now earning, I would not do it.

Sorry girls but lets be honest here; these shows are not at all artistic. To my mind there is no merit in taking off a bra and a 'g string and wrapping it around a man's face, or in sticking your tits in his beer. In the old burlesque days stripping *was* an art. Those girls could take it all off and never show a thing. I went down really well at a good few of these shows and was always treated like the lady I was, by the very gents who had booked these girls. But after doing a couple of shows, one of which involved a snake around which the exotic dancer 'danced' slipping on its shit as it writhed about her private parts and another that required the use of the snout of an innocent teddy bear, I refused to do another one after that.

So it was with surprise I turned up to the Yeoman's Arms in Staffordshire one night to find it was an all male night. I was furious. I had had an extraordinary night there a few weeks previously doing the Roy Castle show. He was wonderful. What a nice man. I met him when he popped his head around my dressing room door to ask me if I would be so kind as to not put up my PA system but to use his. This was because he needed to use the entire floor to tap dance on. He told me I could set the spare channel on his rig to whatever setting I required and he even provided me with a first class mike. No airs, no graces, no edge, just a thoroughly nice man who thanked me for my total co-operation by buying me and my companion a drink. It had been a good show and on the strength of it the Yeoman had booked me privately for this night. But like I said, it was an all male night. I went in search of the manager, needing to shake him by the throat! He reassured me there were no strippers on the show just me and Bernard Manning.

Now I had worked with this nationally acclaimed comedian and a couple of times before and he had a habit of turning his shows into stag shows as the women found his aggressive humour a little hard to take. Backstage he was a surprisingly warm and tender guy who only had to be told your name once and he had you for life. I went into his dressing room and said hello. He asked after my girls and my hubby and bought me a drink. I had to smile. He was mending the gusset of a pair of tan coloured pants with a darning needle thread with black cotton. His stitches were massive. I took it from him and did the job properly. He asked did he need to put up his own gear or could he use mine, a request made by every comic I ever worked with. Since these things are the tools of our trade one doesn't really like to loan them out but me being me, no question. The manager outlined the running of the show; I was to go on and do my part, then there would be a break for the lads to have a prepaid meal and then Bernard was to end the show. That was not on Bernard said.

"I know Joy's work and I know she will do a good job warning them up. Then they sit down to eat and I have to come out cold and start warning them up all over again. It's daft. They need to eat now and then we can run the show continuously after each other."

The manager refused as the meal was planned and those times could not be altered. He insisted on the show being done as he had asked but again the manager said no.

There are times when you have to throw your act out of the window and entertain to suit the circumstances and this was one of them! There was no way these lads were going to politely listen whilst I prettily sang. I chose a full length gown I had made myself. I still have it; it's made of a pretty busy blue patterned cloth and has seen some use in its day. (There is a piccie of me wearing this dress in the second book.) It has a halter neck with a long tie down the back. Now it is very easy for naughty fingers to tug on it and leave me embarrassed. Gotta think like they do folks! So I double safety pinned it *and* the zip into place, now the only way to embarrass me was to cut it and that was not going to happen. I went on stage and worked the floor going in between all the tables and playing up to them. There was the inevitable tug on the strings and zip but they held! I did Dick Emery's entire act that night and had them whooping with laughter! As I raced into the dressing room after the show I demanded to know how long I had done. Not doing my own act, I had no way of timing it and I deliberately did not wear a watch when I worked as I found it irritating when artistes looked at their wrists as though keen to be done. I had done just over an hour.

I went through to the restaurant and sat down to eat the meal so kindly given to me. I ate quickly as I wanted to see Bernard work. Again there is a trick to this; in a room full of men, they will not take readily to a woman being in the room. If they have to look at her and see if she finds it amusing first, it tends to put them off and so I had to secrete myself behind a pillar at the back of the room. The room is an odd shaped one to work. There is (or was...I am talking many many years ago,) a high stage, which looks down on a sizeable dance floor surrounded by tables and chairs. To the left is a large bar, to the right is a sort of alcove that stretches far back and does not have a clear view of the stage. It was packed solid, every chair being taken by a bus trip full of Scottish lads. The meal was just about over and the waiters were barely clearing away the tables when Bernard Manning took it upon himself to pick up my mike and begin his show. He got instant attention. He had them in the palm of his hand throwing out one line gags so fast that had the audience laughing so much they missed the next joke. Then someone in the alcove wanted a drink.....

To be fair, it was not his fault. He tried to bob down so as not to get in the line of vision of the folks behind him as he headed for the bar. But unfortunately Bernard was working the floor and was very close to the bar! He called the man a 'fat bastard' and told him to get off the floor. The man objected and had a stand up argument as to how he had the nerve to call *him* fat! The guys trying to watch the show yelled at the man to sit down, the men in the alcove stood up and told *them* to sit down and shut up and then all hell broke loose. It was the battle of Bannockburn all over again! Bottles, blood and teeth went flying everywhere! I high tailed it back to my dressing room as the fight raged on. After about half an hour, some sort of order was bought about and the manager announced that he would now fetch Bernard back on again. He came on but briefly and told the lads he didn't need their money this bad, his fee for the night was £400 and they could keep it and give it to charity. He earned a fortune from his ELS advert (whatever happened to them?) and had taken a standing ovation in Las Vegas. With that he left the stage and all hell broke loose again!

The manager came to me in a panic and asked me to go back on and do a second spot and he would double my fee. I did. When I came off, I asked him where Bernard was. Afraid for his beautiful car (a Rolls Royce I believe.) he had climbed out of the lavatory window and had gone. I asked what they were going to do with his fee but the manager said his contract insisted he be paid before he even went on stage! I worked with Bernard again several times and we often chuckled at the memory of that night.

The no stripper show ban I imposed though was broken once and it just so happened to be on a night I recall taking Cindy with me to a booking in Stoke on Trent. It unfortunately coincided with her 13th or 14th birthday. At that age, kids usually do their own thing with their own friends but for some reason she had no plans and I offered to take her with me and we would stop on the way home and go to The Chateau on Wilford Lane for a celebratory meal. When we got to the club, to my horror I found it was a stag. Booked through an agent who booked through an agent ad infinitum, the venue was not aware that I didn't do stags. Unfortunately I had little choice in the matter and had to do the job.

But what was I to do about Cindy? Well the only thing we could do was leave her in my dressing room having made her comfy, she most certainly could not view the show and at least we did not have to share a room with the rest of the girls. Now here's a little something else you are about to find out with regard to this side of the entertainment business! The contracts give a starting time which **MUST** be adhered to, but the finishing time is always a bit vague no, in fact it's rarely if ever mentioned. You can assume that its normal drinking hours but if it's a nightclub, you can often not even go on stage until midnight and yet have been contracted to have your gear set up on stage by 7pm! You may then be unable to take down your PA until the last 'act' has done his or her spot, so two and three am exits are not unheard of. This was pretty near one of those nights. My poor young daughter had to sit in that awful room for a good few hours although we did manage to get away by midnight, but when we finally got back to Nottingham and made for The Chateau, it was closed! I'm sure we made it up to her though in the end.

164

CHAPTER THIRTEEN

PHYLLIS!

Zoe was due to start school and I went through a bad patch once she had. I felt quite useless, unwanted, wasted, and redundant and was seriously scared of slipping back into depression. The house was unusually quiet and I didn't know what to do with myself and my spirits only lifted when the kids came home from school and gloom descended again each morning on their departure. Eventually I went to my doctors and asked for help. I saw Doctor Chisholm, our local and also the Nottingham Police Authority doctor. He was a wonderful caring man. He asked a few questions of me then asked how old Zoe was these days. I told him and he nodded his head sagely, a wry grin turning his lips up a little. He excused himself, went into the other room and spoke into his telephone. Although I could see him, I could not hear him. He wrote something down on a note pad, tore it off, came back, handed it to me and said;
"Here's a little job for you. I know you love babies, so you'll love this."

The note was a phone number and the following Monday I began doing voluntary work for the WRVS every Monday Wednesday and Friday morning helping to run the refreshment bar at the City hospital maternity department. And here it was that I met Phyllis Scott...or Phyl as she liked to be called. She was tall, quite stout and ever enveloped from head to toe in her maroon WRVS uniform which she wore with great pride. She had a round shiny wrinkle less face framed with grey wispy hair that she pulled into a bun at the nape of her neck but it had a way of escaping and tiny little curls would stray annoyingly onto her face and she would brush them away testily. She was 68, arthritic and relied heavily on the aid of a pair of sticks. I learned that her much loved husband had died some eight years previous and to talk of him was to open her wounds and tears would readily flow.

We were as different as it was possible to be, in age, life style, fashion, size, values ...etc. But I loved her. I got to know her very well and sometimes when she specifically asked, I began to pick her up but *always* took her home to her massive detached house, the back of which backed onto Perry Road almost opposite the Nottingham prison. Very often she would put lunch on for us and we would sit out in her charming garden and eat it in the warm sunshine. She had two children, Michael and Margaret, both of whom were professional people neither of whom lived at home. I listened for hours to her stories of days gone by. She harked back many times to her young life when she had married. Her bridesmaid had been her old school friend Mary and she was gutted when this friend met and married a Canadian soldier stationed over here during the war. Within months she'd left these shores forever. They had kept in touch she told me, but nothing more than a card or a letter now and then at Christmas and birthdays. Gradually I gleaned how lonely she was and whilst my breakfast pots lay waiting my attention at home, I idled away many a pleasant hour at her side and worked with her for well over a year.

The hospital tea shop was small, claustrophobic even but I got to know all the mums and their bumps personally and took a great interest in them. Then when they had their babies, it was as if they were my own family almost. Dr Chisholm was a wise old man, he was right, I loved this job. Nine out of ten times, I would get in before Phyl and would have it up and running as soon as she arrived. It was only a few hundred yards from where she lived and she liked to walk there as it gave her a bit of exercise, only accepting my offer of a lift in if it was bad weather. I can see her now struggling through the door on her sticks her face shiny with two high spots of red on her cheeks from the exertion. But one day was to be different.

She arrived and struggled in on her sticks as usual but there was something clearly wrong.
"Phyl" I asked, concerned, "what's wrong?"
She shook her head and tears began to flow. Unable to speak she gave me a letter to read. It had a Canadian stamp.

Dear Phyl,
It is with deep regret I have to tell you that Mary is in hospital and is not expected to make a recovery. She did not want to worry you and so did not tell you how ill she was but she is very frail and has been in a wheel-chair for much of this year. A few days ago, the doctors told me she had gone into a coma and would not come out of it again. I spend every hour at the hospital by her side. She does not stir, she doesn't even know me. It's so sad.
I hope this finds you in better health that I am right now.
Kindest regards
Dave Gardener.

I put my arms around her as she sobbed and her tears were on and off all morning. At the end of our shift, I accompanied her home, sat with her through her reminiscences as we looked through her wedding photos of them both as very pretty young ladies. On the Friday I again got to the clinic without her and when she turned in immediately asked after Mary. David had written again and once more she showed me the letter;

My Dear Phyl,

Thank you for your letter and for replying so promptly, it's really appreciated. It was a ray of light in my dark world. She is no better and the doctor tells me she will never wake again and even if she did, she would not recognise me. I sit there by her side for hours on end. When the nurses eventually chuck me out in the early hours of the morning, I go home and then cannot sleep as I feel guilty that I am not by her side. What if she was to wake up and not see me there? We have barely been apart for one day of our entire lives together.
Please stay in touch.

Kindest regards

David.

It was the time of year we took our family holiday and we went abroad for almost three weeks. We had planned two, but for some reason the airline could not get us back on our departure date and so they informed us we would have to stay an extra five days, for which they would pay the bill and also give us spending money. They gave us free use of the phone to call our work and family and we settled down to another few days swimming, eating, sleeping and generally enjoying ourselves. Life can be so hard at times!

Returning to the clinic, I set it up as usual and waited for Phyl to arrive. But I was to get the shock of my life when she did walk through the door. She was upright and ram rod straight. . But I stood there rooted to the spot holding the letters, utterly dumbstruck, unable to take my eyes off her. Unspoken questions came to mind thick and fast...where was her uniform? She had on a white blouse, white floral skirt and white cardigan and whose were those white fancy sandals she was wearing? When had she had her hair cut, styled and coloured, *COLOURED*? WHY WAS SHE WEARING PINK LIPSTICK? **AND IN HEAVENS NAME, WHERE WERE HER STICKS?** She spoke making me jump.

"Hello Joy, did you have a good holiday? I got your card." she smiled, her eye's lighting up.

I finally found my stuttering voice.

"Wh where. are your sticks?"

"I've decided I don't need them anymore, I can walk perfectly well without them." she said matter of factly and she could.

"Ohh, wh...why are you wearing lipstick?"

I finally spat it out. She was immediately on the defensive.

"'Good morning Phyl, oh yes thank you, we had a lovely holiday, how kind of you to ask, I'm glad you got the card I sent you and how are you? And while I think about it, where were you last week?'"

"Oh Phyl, sorry, the flight was cancelled and we had to stay on for almost another week. I am sorry, it's just that you

169

you...look so, so... so different, so nice and where is your uniform?" I finished lamely.

"Don't stare at me like that. I often wear lipstick and as it's a nice sunny day I decided not to wear my uniform, I do *have* other clothes you know, I don't actually sleep in that thing. Besides, I am going into town to get a photograph taken, ok?"

"Yes of course it's ok and I love your hair, you look lovely....why are you having your photo taken?"

"Dave wants me to get one done to send to him. Anyway its time we were open." *Dave* is it now?

"How are they?"

Her eyes clouded over for a few seconds as she fumbled in her bag and thrust a sheaf of letters into my hands.

"Here, read these."

She turned and finished wiping down the worktops prior to opening up the café.

"Do you really want me to read these?" I queried.

"Yes. There's nothing in there I need be ashamed of."

I looked down at the letters, they were placed in date order and there were quite a few. I opened the first one; it began Dear Phyl and was a nothing more than a brief report on the unchanged condition of his wife.

"Oh poor thing, tut, poor both of them."

"Carry on reading you are in for a surprise."

The rattle of the shutters signified the end for now of the conversation and I buried myself in the letters as she busied herself with the customers. The next one began My Dear Phyl, then My Dearest Phyl, each one getting more and more personal. I'd got about halfway through them when I came across his photo. Although old, he was handsome if a little craggy in the face, with a thick head of dark grey hair whiter at the temples. He was wearing what looked to be a leather waistcoat over a checked lumber shirt and had on a thin leather thong around his neck which had a silver cattle head skull decoration pulling the thong tight to his throat. I turned my attention to this letter and read how he told of the doctor taking Dave into his room, sitting him down and giving him a good talking to.

The gist of it was that Mary was never going to wake up and see him again, that he had not many good years left of his own life and he should not waste his time sitting by her bed, he being absolutely certain it would not be what she wanted for him and to go and do whatever he wanted to before it was too late. He confessed in this letter that what the doctor had said had really opened his eyes and he realised he wanted to come and see England one last time. She had seemingly replied that she would love to see him again.....Each letter I read had become more and more affectionate and personal until finally they began My Darling Phyl and there I stopped as they seemed to be too personal for my eyes.

We didn't speak much for the rest of the day and as she was going into town, I went straight home. By the time the next shift came round, it was cut and dried, he was on his way to England and was due to arrive the next night. Margaret had arranged to have time off work and she would accompany her mother to Heathrow airport to meet him. He was booked into the Westminster Hotel at the bottom of Mansfield road and he would stay as long as he needed, Phyl having agreed to accompany him on his wanderings and so she had booked a fortnight's holiday from the WRVS.

I continued to work in her place over those two weeks and at one point they did send a replacement for her but we didn't hit it off and she only came the once. A fortnight later, I went to the tea shop as usual, set everything up and waited for Phyl to come. The door opened and in she walked. At least I thought it was her; *she looked so different.* She was taller, tons slimmer, younger looking and some indefinable something had slipped from her shoulders leaving her looking relaxed and happy. And then she told me;

She knew she had made a mistake as soon as they got to the airport. Silently she screamed at herself asking what the hell had she been thinking. They stood and waited as the flight arrival from Canada was announced over the tannoy. Then suddenly he was walking towards her, the living image of his photo, still wearing the leather string tie round his neck and pushing his suitcase on a trolley. To be fair, his photo had not done him justice; he was still a handsome man. She didn't care what he looked like, she just wished the floor would open up and swallow her and she felt sick. He was about twenty five yards away, almost at her side when a tannoy message came over;

"Would Mr David Gardener of flight CA 429 please go to British Airways desk immediately?"

He stopped, paled and panicked. Phyl raced to his side, took his arm and guided him over to the information desk where he was asked to produce his passport to check he was the right man they were looking for. They gave him the news from the hospital to say that as he was flying over here, his wife had died. He was inconsolable and full of guilt. Phyl and Margaret helped him to her car and they made for home. The journey was long and tedious and he barely spoke.

When they got home, he relaxed a little and they talked and talked until it got very late. Margaret stood up and said she had to go as she had an early start tomorrow and would he like a lift to his hotel? He declined saying he was jet lagged, not at all sleepy and would get a taxi. It seems he never used the hotel and they married a few months later. My family and I were invited but in the meantime we had again booked a holiday and were away.

I was so sorry to have missed it. A few months later, they moved away to a bungalow in Lincoln. I visited them once, but it was too far to go and with my family and busy lifestyle we were reduced to the occasional phone call until we lost touch altogether and I never heard from them again. I hope they had a long and very happy life together.....

CHAPTER FOURTEEN

CENTRAL TELLY!

Back on the home front we 'artistes' were getting tremendously excited. We'd been told by Jack Denman that a TV company was to be set up in Nottingham and it seemed no sooner had it been thought of than it happened and a lot of the technical, wardrobe and make-up staff moved from London to a specially built studio on Lenton Lane. To some of the staff it was a godsend. The simple terraced houses they owned in London were sold for astronomical amounts of money and even the most died in the wool Londoners who may well have been loathe to leave found they were able to buy near mansions for the same price here. It didn't take long for the work to filter through to us and in 1981 I was offered my first job. The phone rang....

"Joy James?"

"Yes."

"Jack Denman here, dear. There is a couple of days work going on the new adaptation of Son's and Lovers. It's on a set in Derbyshire on the forecourt of the Dixie's Arms pub, there's a few others going so I will get one of them to pick you up and you can share the driving costs."

This was to be my first ever TV experience, I was to be a pub waitress and was wildly excited.

The Dixie's Arms is halfway down a steep hill and had been turned back into what it would probably have looked like in Lawrence's day, if you can ignore the double glazed windows! The forecourt had been set dressed as if for a fete and gala with masses of red white and blue bunting colourfully decorating the pub frontage, the fencing and every tree. Large trestle tables were laid out and folk dressed in drab Victorian garb were milling about. They had kitted me out in an authentic corset over which was a dowdy costume with several skirts and high black leather ankle boots with a huge nail sticking straight into my heel. It was a lovely day and high in the trees above us vast amounts of rooks wheeled and cawed.

Each person had his or her job to do and this could be simply walking in front of the camera or sitting quaffing flagons of ale in the warm sunshine. As the waitress, I had to emerge from within the pub with two huge heavy wicker baskets full of loaves of bread and a red and white chequered tablecloth. I had to spread the cloth on the table, set down the baskets of bread on it, go back inside and return with two huge stone jugs of ale.

"Aaaannnd....ACTION."

I hauled the heavy baskets of bread out of the pub, walked briskly across the car park and set them down on a stool, I then undid the folds of the cloth and threw it over the table. I was just lifting up the first basket when I heard a moped come 'putt putt putting' down the hill. I also heard for the first time in my life those well known words;

"CUT...ANNND RESET," resignedly bellowed down a megaphone.

I picked up the tablecloth, folded it carefully, put it in one of the baskets and hauled them both back into the pub.

"Aaaannnddd....ACTION."

I repeated my earlier actions and stiffly walked out of the pub, dumped the bread baskets on the stool, unfolded the cloth threw it on the table, lifted up the first basket of bread and a very un Victorian police car came racing down the hill, sirens blaring.

"CUT...ANNND RESET!" the tone never varying. I undid all my actions again and patiently and somewhat painfully returned to my start position. By now the nail in my shoe was doing some damage but hey, this was my first job and there was no way I would make a name for myself as a whiner.

"Aaaannndddd....ACTION."

I limped out of the back, put my bread on the stool, undid the tablecloth threw and straightened it into place and lifted first one basket of bread, then the second one. I held my breath and hobbling painfully back inside the pub, picked up the two stone flagons of beer and headed for the table again. I had almost made it when a small dumpy guy in a grey lounge suit with a glass of whiskey in his hands, walked out of the pub, crossed my path, stood stock still in the middle of the set and asked what we were doing?

"CUT...ANNND RESET!"

How does the man keep his temper? It took me even longer this time as I had got the ale flagons to take back too, but I winced my bloodied foot through the re-set action and went back to my start position.

"Aaaannndddd....ACTION."

Again I almost made it to the table with the flagons of ale when a jet screamed overhead.

"CUT...ANNND RESET!"........the man has the patience of a saint I decided.

This happened again and again and again until I could no longer hold it in and I screeched;

"This bleeding tables been laid more times than I have!"

The whole set collapsed into fits of laughter and those few

words one day in the not too distant future, would be remembered and earn me an unexpected bonus!

When he had finished laughing Stuart Burge the director told us to go and get our lunches and we would try again later on. When we got back on the set after lunch we found the bloody rooks had eaten all the bread! When the finished programme was shown on the TV, I excitedly looked for myself naturally. I saw what could have been my left leg in one shot, certainly my right shoulder was identifiable in another (is this where the phrase 'bit part actor' came from?) and there was definitely a full length back view of me limping painfully into the pub. So this was *fame*?

My next job came hot on the heels of the first one. This took place in Mapperley and was a modern day wedding scene for a programme called Inside Out. The house we filmed in was truly beautiful. It had a sloping garden that had been cleverly stepped into several little gardens and was beautifully manicured and landscaped. Along the bottom ran a reception table dressed in a white tablecloth decorated with magnificent fresh flowers and loaded with a vast amount of crystal glasses, bottles of Dom Perignon champagne and a beautiful notwithstanding cardboard wedding cake.

Two of our lads determined that they would have a bottle of the champers spirited away before the day was over. I knew what was going on and it was fun to watch them nearly do it time and time again, but something always managed to stop them. Nevertheless, at the end of the day, despite them moving the other bottles to disguise the fact, I noticed there was one missing. Their hard work had paid off it seemed. It's normal on these sets to be addressed by the floor manager at the end of the days shoot, or 'wrap' as it's colloquially called. This is usually to thank us for our efforts or even to tell us we'd be needed the following day for 'continuity'. To be 'needed' again the following day is cause to raise your head in triumph a little higher than that of your working companions whose services will *not* be needed!

On this occasion the director added at the end of his speech that that he hoped whoever had stolen the bottle of champagne would have the sense to chill it first as tap water is so much better ice cold! I knew it was Mike who'd had that bugger and looked across at him. He looked as sick as the proverbial parrot! As we left for the night, I noticed a familiar unopened bottle stuffed under the neatly clipped cotoneaster hedge.

There are no hard and fast rules about doing extra work...except one! *You can be pretty damned certain that if you are required to (say) be dressed in winter boots with a heavy fur coat and a smothering fleeced hood, the shot will be done on the hottest day of the year!* Conversely, if you need to be dressed prettily in a flowery summer number, be bare legged with peep toed high heeled shoes, it will be shot on the coldest day of the year, usually in the middle of January. This was one of the many days' shoots I did on different episodes of Shine on Harvey Moon. The scene was shot at the Loughborough steam railway station which had been dressed to replicate the war time Liverpool Street station in London. It was a beautifully sunny but bitterly *bitterly* cold day.

Authenticity is paramount on these shoots and I was dressed in a sleeveless light blue cotton flowered 1940's utility dress, my legs having been coloured by having gravy powder rubbed onto them and with heels and seams drawn on in eyebrow pencil. My freezing cold feet had been shoved into whacking high wedged heeled shoes and my hair had been done up in the 'victory roll' style of the day. I was given some fancy short lace gloves I could either wear or carry a brown leather shoulder bag and a suitcase. The train was to steam in, Kenneth Cranham (Harvey Moon) was to run up and down the platform frantically looking for someone on it and I was required to alight from the train carrying my suitcase, walk past him and carry on the length of the station and out of shot. I asked wardrobe had they got a cardigan I could wear but I was told it was a very hot day and I had to be bare armed. Hot? Can't say I'd noticed. I tried the make up girls and pointed out that my bare arms were now deeply and angrily mottled and wouldn't this show? But they said it would look like sun tan on the finished shot! Purple sun tan?

We'd had it drilled into us we must not go anywhere to the right as in the real Liverpool Street station this was just a brick wall. Over and over again we were told not to turn right. And *I* didn't but then I wasn't required to go in that direction anyway. The cold numbs the brain and we had to cut and re-set so many times as people inadvertently walked into the virtual 'wall'. Some of the more fortunate people that day had to merely sit in costume on the wonderfully warm train as it came in, or sit in a heated waiting room.

Not me. This scene took hours and hours to do and each reset saw me dive into the nearest carriage - never the same one twice - to grab a little warmth. On the first reset, I lost my gloves, the second saw my handbag disappear, the third my suitcase. Continuity is EVERYTHING to the editors of these programmes. Nothing was more important to them than this but nothing was more important to me that day than getting a bit of warmth into my frozen bones.

If anyone noticed the missing objects they said nothing. In the next shot, I was dressed in a thick warm coat but the shot was done in darkness in the early hours of the morning. I think it took me about a week to properly thaw out! When that episode was shown on the TV, I think I saw a ('bit part') of my 'Victory roll' hair-do but bugger all else! I went on to do quite a few different episodes of this show including one wherein I was a magistrate and sat on the bench in the Nottingham City council house. Have you ever been in there? What a place it is, its elegance is almost beyond words. During a break in filming, I did my usual, went walk about in solitude and felt privileged to be able to really enjoy its beauty.

Another job came in whilst I was on holiday in Corfu and due to plane delays we had not got back until the early hours. My answer-phone was flashing and I clicked it on. There was a message from Jack Denman telling me I was booked the next morning on Harvey Moon. It warranted a 5am start. I groaned it was hardly worth me going to bed. It was an incredible day in that not only did we have that early start but we weren't due to wrap until 2am the next day. Fortunately there was no long haul to the venue, just a short hop across town, For once, luck was with me as it was a summer shot and I was simply required to sit on a bus for the first shot. What could be easier?

The bus – a genuine 1940's one – had to trundle along a Radford street a stones throw away from my first ever marital home, past dozens of terraced houses, turn a corner, and as it slowed to go into the turn, Harvey Moon jumped off the bus platform and walked jauntily down another street full of three up three down terraced houses. What could possibly go wrong? What could possibly go right? On the first run a

180

women opened up her lounge window and hung out, dressed in her 1980's clothes. 'AND CUT!' The inevitable police siren, the real honest to goodness modern day bus, the tinkle of an ice cream van, the lost taxi...I could go on and on....

There had been warnings that this scene really should be hurriedly shot before the kids came out of school, but the powers that be were not listening or maybe there were too many interruptions and all too soon the kids came out of school.... Ye gods. The little buggers raced around the streets chasing the bus on their bikes, they raided the food that had been set out for our tea, they stole all the boxes of fruit juice and the cream cake trays bore nothing but a mere few icing crumbs; folk started to come home from their work and parked their 1980's model Fords outside the houses and were loathe to move them. The wheels on the bus went round and round, round and round....its 1940's engine droned monotonously on and on and on.... CUT...RE-SET...CUT...RE-SET.... I fell sound asleep and no-one woke me when the bus finally stopped and I had a good couple of hours of much needed zedding whilst they had their tea!

I can remember quite a lot of jobs that were set in the depths of winter and which were truly terrible to do. How about Jenny's War? Yes how about Jenny's War! This was another 1940's epic, a true story of an American mother (Dyan Cannon) whose pilot son (a very young Hugh Grant) goes missing and she sets out to find him by dressing herself up as a man and going into war torn Germany. Its stars were impressive, also including Elke Sommer, Robert Hardy, Nigel Hawthorne, Christopher Casenove, Richard Todd and Michael Elphick but there was a horrible undercurrent running through the whole shoot. What it boiled down to was the old adage 'too many cooks spoil the broth'. It was a combined US/Harlech TV production and what one director wanted the other one queried, this led to friction that filtered down through the ranks and ended up on we extra's shoulders. Ask any 'extra' which job they hated the most and they will undoubtedly say Jenny's War. The conditions we worked in were truly appalling.

The one good thing about all film shoots is the way you are looked after with regard to your physical well being. All meals are provided and are without exception, superb. Breakfast will be every item known to man from porridge to cereals to kippers through to full English. Oh man, those wonderful delicious fried brekkies first thing on a cold morning.... ohhhh. Mid morning there is coffee and biscuits, lunch the best you can imagine. Oh where do I begin? There are several starters, every salad, fruit and cold meat known to man, three or four main courses and a waist thickening array of puddings, cheeses sweets and chocolates. Tea is tray after tray of every combination of sandwich you can think of. There's always banana and crunchy brown sugar, tuna and mayo, corned beef and pickle, cheese and onion, (getting hungry? I wonder why!) Pork and apple sauce, chicken and stuffing, egg and cress, ham and mustard, roast beef and horseradish, smoked salmon spread and cream cheese, and then tray upon tray of home made cream cakes to die for or to give up your diet for. Supper if you are on a late shoot is hot wholesome soup, fish and chips, bowls of steaming hot curry, garlic bread and thick nutmeg crusted rice puddings and all this is prepared and cooked in what is little more than a caravan sized mobile kitchen. These catering companies are our hero's.

To begin with, we were to be picked up by bus promptly at 5am. When I got there bang on time, there were very few people on it. The bus driver had been told he had to pick up so many here and then go onto another pick-up point and yet onto another one or two. There is always someone who is late. So we sat that morning outside the Playhouse in town and waited for the latecomer. Once again it was in the bitter depths of winter and was dark and horribly cold, a ground hoar frost glistening in the street lights. I remember Bobby Charles was on that job that morning and he was joined by a chatterbox. Now I have to tell you here and now, nobody is anybodies friend at that unearthly time of day. I am not a nasty tempered person in the mornings, just very quiet and am fine unless you torment me, then all hell will break loose I promise you. Bobby Charles is a really nice guy whom I have known forever. The chatterbox started as soon as he sat down.

"Ah went ter Hucknall flea market last night. It were a good 'un."

"Hummm..." muttered Bobby in a placid gentle way. I would have killed the chatterbox.

"Ev yer ever bin?"

"Hummm..." he mumbled, again calm and tolerant.

"Its in the market place in Hucknall, do ya know Hucknall?"

"Hummm" said Bobby; his tone never wavered as the dawn cold turned his breath to vapour.

"Its like a car boot really more than a flea market but yo'll never guess what ah got there.."

"A flea?"

Oh come on, crack your face, I did, for 5am I thought that pretty good. Just sitting and waiting was bad enough but what should have taken about an hour took nearly three before the last one got on board. On the bus, with us all huddled together, it wasn't so bad, damp and muggy but bearable. The driver told us we could not go on the set and he was to park in Clipstone Forest.

As we'd picked up more people it became like 'old home' week in that we met up with fellow actors and artistes from other parts of the county whom we'd probably not seen for years maybe and so there was a lot of catching up to do and as the hours went on there was the usual laughter and bon homie. Over the next few hours the conversation dripped away to nothing but monosyllabic mutterings. Some snoozed, some drew Marjorie Proop like images on the steamy windows, others read papers or books, or did cross words or knitted. The weather was appalling. It rained non stop, that horrid fine rain that wets you through and makes the day so dark that even getting off the bus to stretch your legs was not a pleasant option.

The only thing that kept us going that awful first day of our weeks booking on Jenny's War was the thought of the hot food we would soon be tucking into, having missed breakfast by hours due to the late comers. Lunch is invariably 1pm on the dot. It came and went and every minute after that seemed like an hour. Then at about 1.30pm one of the production cars came alongside the bus and the driver opened up the boot. Inside were several dozen pre-packed picnic boxes and these were given to our driver to pass along to us. Inside was two small bread rolls, a couple of processed cheese triangles, a packet of Quavers, a small piece of commercially wrapped fruitcake, a pappy apple and a tiny thick horrible fruit drink. Lunch had been served. We were still on the bus when teatime came round and that was a packet of biscuits and a different but just as sickly fruit drink. Ugh!

Finally, in the fast darkening pm, we were needed and were driven to the set which was massed around two small bridges. Under one, Dyan Cannon was sat enveloped and comforted in a huge white duvet surrounded by industrial sized Calor gas heaters which blew hot air onto her. Someone spotted the food wagon and we all sidled over to it, diving on the cups and getting a much needed hot drink and helping ourselves to the remains of the sandwiches. The canteen lads saw what we had done and viciously bollocked us. Then we were positioned for our shoot. We had to form a long queue and go through a 'check point' which was supposedly under this bridge. The American director rather fatuously told us we were refugee's who had been waiting here for hours and to look miserable. Believe me it took no acting. If we had been cold and miserable that day it was yet to get even worse. As the director called ACTION they turned water hoses on us to make it look as though it was driving rain and we stood and shuffled forwards, we stood and shuffled, stood and shuffled, stood.....

In the next scene Miss Cannon had to stand in the queue with us as the 'Commandant' announced that everyone would be subjected to a thorough search. Miss Cannon was pretending to be a man and was about to be found out. One of her male friends would come round the corner in an old rattling truck and loudly exhorted her to jump on the running board and they'd race off into the night whilst the German soldiers fired wildly after them. She was quite rightly afraid to do this shot. Everywhere was sopping wet through and muddy and she felt she could slip under the wheels and be seriously hurt. And whilst she and the director discussed the scene, we stood in the heavy 'rain'... They put some sackcloth onto the running board to give her some foot grip but she was still afraid. And still we stood in the heavy 'rain'... Finally, they decided to do the whole thing in slow motion and speed it up when they edited it. And we stood; take after take after miserable take, waiting in the heavy 'rain'.....

I had done a job like this once before in which I had to be drenched from head to foot due to a fire extinguisher going off as we did the conger for a TV series called Tales of Sherwood Forest starring Pete Postlethwait. It was a studio shot and when the tons of water had been dropped everyone else was told to hurry to their dressing rooms where warm towelling gowns and hair dryers were waiting. I was drenched yet again and continued with my lines to end the shot. When I was cleared by the director, I hurried off and found the promised warm dressing gown and a pile of towels. Like I say, they really do look after you so well...except on the Jenny's War production!

The next day when we turned up at 5am, we had to put those awful clothes back on again and they were sodden. Don't forget this was a freezing cold November. We did five horrible days on it though it seemed much longer and then, because it was a dual production, for some reason we got paid peanuts. I don't know if I am seen in it, I can honestly say hand on heart I have never watched it. Funny that!

CHAPTER FIFTEEN

BEATING ENNUI

One film I really did enjoy being involved in was Little Lord Fauntleroy starring among others, Alec Guinness and Ricky Schroeder and the booking was for both me and my youngest daughter Zoe aged about nine or ten at the time. It was filmed at Belvoir Castle, a place I am not unfamiliar with having taken my children there many times on day outings. For this occasion it was closed to all but the film crew and actors for the duration and it was a no expense spared sumptuous production set in the most beautiful surroundings.

Extra work is unbelievably tiring, not in any *physical* way, its just jaw achingly boring to simply stand and wait and we can stand and wait for hours and hours on end. There are exceptions to that rule. If like me you are lucky enough to be booked for a day or two's work on something starring Ricky Tomlinson, bored you are not going to be. Out comes the cards! I love cards and would play Coon Can daily if I could. Ricky invited me into this newly set up card school and we sat for hours. I lost, but not a lot, I gained the experience of being in his delightful if somewhat forthright company.

But getting back to Little Lord Fauntleroy....I had been lucky this particular day and had been coiffed and be-gowned into my 'role' as a Christmas dinner guest the minute I had alighted from the bus and had already done my shot and now waited for the much loved words IT'S A WRAP FOLKS! But I knew that to be many hours hence. I knew it was set to be a long and tedious day. Zoe was off somewhere being filmed and I was getting bored stiff.

If anyone attached to that house is reading this, they will now go into a cold sweat and have a dickey fit. I took it upon myself to go off for an exploratory walk. There was no one to stop me and I walked through corridor after corridor, room after room of the house, opening doors that had notices boldly shouting PRIVATE, DO NOT ENTER. I stepped carefully over the red silken ropes and looked closely at the riches I had admired so often from a few yards back. But up close and personal now, I could examine the very brush strokes on the priceless paintings, see the intricate silk stitchery on the soft furnishings, stand almost nose to nose with the miniature portraits hanging either side of the vast marble fireplace and even lean into bookcases containing rich leather bound books close enough to pick up a scent rarer than any other on earth. Aware of the damage just touching can do, I had till now resisted the urge to lay my hands on anything that I could conceivably damage but awestruck I added to the sheen by touching the foot of a marble statue as countless thousands of others before me had felt compelled to do. I explored room after sumptuous room, floor after spectacular floor eventually landing up in the kitchen.

It was damn near the size of a football pitch. The floor was of large age greyed flag stones and our mam would have loved the black leaded fireplace on one wall that was longer than our entire Moffat Street house. In its hearth stood a spit on which would have been roasted whole cattle and the ovens either side were massive. Down the centre of the room was the biggest scrubbed topped, oak table I had or have ever seen. It was monstrous. From side to side and end to end, it was covered in food and not just any old food, the very very best you can imagine. I told you this was a no expense spared production and here, if I needed it, was the proof.

There were two suckling pigs which had been used as a centrepiece for the middle of the dining table. Each one was sat on a tray of greenery and dressed lavishly with shiny red apples stuck in their mouths. Other green apples had been peeled and blackened over a live flame had then been thinly sliced exposing the pale inner flesh which had then been laid down its back with a slide rule, the slices being interspersed here and there with sliced cucumbers, miniature palm trees made from celery, radishes cut exquisitely into roses and bunches of cherries had been strung together in decorative groups and were hung from its ears. Tucked onto each tail was a Harrods Price tag of £56....THEN!

There were several whole unused chickens, tray after tray of sliced turkey breast and roast pork, a fancily dressed leg of lamb, a couple of large pre roasted sirloins of beef, bags of frozen vegetables, capons and whole dishes of pate's. At the far end, dozens of uncut Christmas cakes and puddings, mince pies and bowl after bowl of exotic fruits so crowded the table that you could not have put down as much as thimble. It was groaning under all that weight.

On the far side of the room, there was a bank of sinks all those old fashioned shallow yellow ones with a lone cold brass tap dripping over each of them and two men were valiantly trying to wash a hundred or more monogrammed plates that had been used in the banqueting scenes. Mam would have felt quite at home stood there. Maybe the men

189

were not used to washing up because they were making a right pig's ear of the job.

"You won't get them greasy plates clean without hot water." I commented.

"There *is* only cold taps and these plates are only the tip of the iceberg, there are dozens more to be fetched from the banqueting table yet and we have to take them back to the props warehouse in London tonight. We'll never be finished in time."

"There are kettles, why not boil a couple and get hot water?"

"We don't know how the cooker works."

Bless, they were only men!

"Oh move over, I'll do it. You two go and fetch the rest."

"Oh you are a love," one said over his shoulder as the two of them were already halfway out of the room.

The brass kettles were huge and I had a momentary vision of the kitchen maids in Victorian times having muscles like boxers. They were heavy even without water and I had all on to lift them once they were filled. I looked under the curtains fronting the sinks hoping to find some washing up liquid but all there was, was a box of Daz soap powder. It would just have to do. I worked steadily for about an hour and the lads came back with another trolley of dirty dishes and disappeared again. I was just wiping and stacking the last few plates when the door opened and a man walked into the kitchen. He greeted me cordially and asked me what I was doing. I explained and he thanked me. It turned out, he was the film crew chef.

"Do you have any children?"

"Yes three girls, why?"

"Because all this.." he swept his hand in a circle to encompass all the food on the table, "..is surplus to

190

requirements and will have to be dumped and it's a crying shame. Would you like to take it home?"

Would I *what*?

I told him I had two fourteen cubic foot freezers at home and could accommodate any amount. He gave me the lot and helped me fill three black bin bags full to the very brim and even helped me carry them to our bus where we stashed them in the boot. One of the more profitable days work I think. The day had been saved for me by being able to wander freely albeit very carefully through the house and also finding something to do did help the inevitable ennui. Tomorrow, I would not be as lucky as I was to be dressed in sombre Victorian attire and was spending much of the day filming in church. I tried taking a book with me but it did nothing to lessen my boredom. Being roughly the same age, my daughter Zoe and Ricky Schroeder had a good day in each others company.

Then as we finally finished for the day I was taken to one side and told they needed Zoe again the next day for a continuity shot. I was reluctant but she pleaded with me and so I went, unaware until I got my pay that I was to get chaperone money too. Free to wear my own clothes I stood and watched the filming. Actor Tony Melody told me I scrubbed up well! A few days later I had another of my parties and served a banquet of my own and in pride of place were two suckling pigs!

A week later I was sent to Lincoln to do a couple of days on Oliver. The set boys had completely reconstructed the streets to look as Victorian as they could. It was amazing what they did with of all things, polystyrene. There was a traffic island in the middle of a road that was vital to filming. So they 'built' a realistic looking Victorian 'iron' water fountain over it and it looked as though it had always been there. Yellow lines were covered up with bags and bags of old dried leaves, whilst some parts of this beautiful city have remained unchanged for eons and so needed no help.

One extra, with 'special skills', was a young man who played the penny whistle and was going to be used in a crowded market scene as a Victorian busker. All day long he practised one tune he called All the Kings Men. I knew the tune off by heart, we ALL knew the tune off by heart. It went something like this;

A tiddly tiddly tiddly too,
a diddly diddly diddly doo.

He played it over and over. At last came his time and the director, bored by hearing that same tune over and over asked him could he play another song. Oh yes he could, it was a song called Ode to the King. He played it and it went something like this;

A tiddly tiddly tiddly too
A diddly diddly diddly doo!

You know how there are different words to the same hymn music.....

At one point in this filming, we had to do something within the cathedral walls and we met a charming American woman who was married to one of the church men and she lived in the cathedral. She took us to places we could not possibly have known of and at one point showed us to a high up walled garden that overlooked the whole city and invited us to pick ripe peaches that were growing there!

CHAPTER SIXTEEN

COBBLERS!

The phone rang and it was he of the dark brown velvet voice.

"Jack Denman here dear, just had a call from Central. They are looking for someone with a local accent to play Bill Maynard's wife in a six week situation comedy for radio Trent. I thought I might put you forward. Are you interested?"

"Do you think I could do it?"

"I *know* you could do it. I wouldn't have faxed your details over to them if I didn't think you could. What's not to do? It's not like TV, you don't have to memorise lines for the radio you know, you read straight off the script."

I respected his knowledge of such things. He hadn't always been an agent. First and foremost he was a trained actor/entertainer who'd worked all over the country including revues in the West End theatres until the outbreak of world war two. The Variety Agency had come about almost by accident a lot later and what he didn't know about the business could have been written on a grain of rice. He had been called up as an entertainer and had been put into a show called The Ace's.

This show and other later shows he was associated with travelled extensively to the Far East, and he entertained in all manner of places, sometimes even behind the front lines and once he even went for tea to the Vice Regal Palace with the Viceroys wife and she persuaded him to do charity shows for her there. He toured India, Burma, Ceylon, Pakistan,

Uzbekistan, Java Sumatra and many other far eastern places. Then he joined ENSA which had been devised as an entertainment section at the outbreak of the 1939 war.

It had originally been set up by Basil Dean and Leslie Henson and you had to be the very cream to be even considered fit to work with them. Knowing his work, they chose Jack to work alongside another chap whose name you might recall, Jack Hawkins and they worked on and put together shows to be played for our forces all over the world. One of the shows was produced specifically for SEAC (South East Asia Command) and it ran for three whole years. After the war, he came back to resume his career but venues were closing all over London and it was only when a dear friend of his, the well known crooner Denny Dennis complained to Jack that he was unable to find work that the idea of starting an agency to help such artistes, came to him. He moved back to the midlands and formed the Denman Variety Agency. This has grown to currently have a database of thousands. So if Jack said he thought me capable of auditioning for stuff like this, who was I to argue?
"I wouldn't want to let you down Jack." I said warily.
"You never have yet my dear" he said encouragingly, as he always did, "the auditions are next Monday. I've put Charlie Bartle, Val Terry and myself forward for it too. I'll put the script and details in the post to you."

They arrived the next day. Basically the story was about a Del boy type character who hi-jacks 'Cobblers', his son's pop band, the leader of the group being played by Bill's real life musician son Maynard Williams. I read it through and thought Jack was right, it *was* something I could do. He rang me back again that day to ask had I got the paperwork, I said yes and he then dropped a bit of a bombshell.

"You'll be up against some stiff competition. I've just found out that the word has spread on the grapevine and the big guns down in London are sending actors up to audition."
Whoa..here come the nerves again right on cue!
"....are you in Equity by the way?"
"No why?"
"Oh, I always assumed you were, only they are a bit sticky about anyone taking work that could be done by bona fide union members."
"Oh that's it then, I am not a bona fide Equity backed actress so that puts me out of the running."
"No, it doesn't, you are working full time in the variety side of the business and you are entitled to join. You need to give Val Terry a call, tell him I sent you and get you signed up and you need to do it today so it's validated before the audition, then nobody can sling any mud."
I got on the phone to Val and he advised me to come into his Mansfield Road office like NOW, which I did. He signed me up immediately, back dating my application by a week just to be on the safe side, but boy did the cost hurt my purse!

It has never been cheap to belong to this particular trade union and it is even more expensive now. I personally think it's too much like our parliamentary set up, far too heavy on the top table, with hundreds of thousands of little fish like me bearing the weight of supporting them all. In the mid 80's I became Treasurer of the East Midlands branch, a post I went on to hold for several years it was nice once a year to go to their AGM in London all expenses paid. There I got to speak to some very well known actors and actresses even if it was only to ask how many sugars they took! And though I didn't actually get to speak to all these luminaries, just to see, hear and breath the same air as them made my day and their impassioned speeches on topics they held dear was theatre enough for me. Frances De La Tour, Vanessa Redgrave, Tony Robinson, Corin Redgrave to name but a few had me enthralled just looking and listening to them. The union always put us up in a decent hotel as we had to stay over. One night there was an almighty bang right beneath my window. With my heart thumping I raced to and opened it. Below me a taxi was on fire. The IRA had struck again. I think that was another night when my sheets had to be changed!

I had been the treasurer of the East Midlands branch of Equity for some considerable time and one night at a meeting one of our members stood up and said that she had been in Equity for over a year and they had just issued her with yet another provisional card. She raised her hand to show the card. Wasn't she entitled to full membership she wanted to know? The secretary said she would look into it for her and the meetings 'any other business' continued. Something about the colour of her card puzzled me. I dived into my handbag and bought out my own card. I interrupted the secretary and said;

"Whilst the secretary looks into your case, maybe she would also like to look into mine. I too merely hold a provisional one and I have been a fully paid-up member for over nine years!"

I only quote this instance to show you how sloppy they could be at times.

In theory membership is supposed to give the members a security blanket that protects their interests and gives them rights to all sorts of legal help if they need it but in practice it can be a very different story. I paid my annual dues *faithfully, albeit begrudgingly, for many years without ever needing, asking for or getting anything back from them other than the previously all important 'card'. By now however, the card wasn't that important as Prime Minister Maggie Thatcher had stopped people being denied work merely because they didn't belong to this union and so didn't have this card. It had been a closed shop for ever and it was ludicrous. In order to get work, you HAD to have the card, but you couldn't get the card unless you had worked in the industry and could prove it. Hello? The day was to come though when I did need Equity's help and it was not to be forthcoming.*

A new agency owned and run by a man named Reid Graham had recently opened up and talk had it, he seemed to have a lot of well paid work. In common with everybody else, I joined his agency. He booked me for a 2 day 'walk on 2' shoot on a new programme which was just getting underway. If you are an extra, you get a certain flat rate of pay, back then it was about £40 net a day. By the time you have taken off your outgoings i.e. travel costs, agency costs – (Jacks never changed from 10% - but the other agencies charged more and Reid Graham was at the higher rate of fee's plus the dreaded vat) it was not worth doing. But 'walk on' 1 2 3 etc based on words or some skill they required and which you had, was much better paid and if you were lucky enough to have to say a few lines, the sky was the limit.

The job he offered me and which I was going for, was a 'walk on 2' which meant I had lines and so it was to pay even more. I told him I would not want to go all that way on my own as I was not the best of drivers having no sense of direction. He told me travel would not be a problem as others were going up too and he would arrange for me to get

197

a lift and share the costs. I was told the only requisite for this job was I had to have long brassy blonde hair, something I didn't have. Waiting until the job was confirmed I then went out and expensively bought a long bright brassy blonde wig knowing that the fee would more than cover its cost. I informed Reid and he in turn told the TV Company and back came the word the wig would be fine and they looked forward to seeing me on the day. The finer details like time and place seemed to be a bit vague and slow in the coming and it was gone 7 on the eve of the job before he finally phoned me with those all important details.

This is not at all unusual. The production team walk a tight rope. If that days shooting goes over time and very often it does, there is a need to continue it the next day so there's no point in booking actors who merely stand around all day, need to be fed and cost them dear only to have to be re-booked for the next day too, so its not unknown for them to wait until its 'a wrap' before turning their attention to the following days work and labour requirements. I now learned the venue was Bispham, top side of Blackpool! He told me no-one else was going that day and I would have to go alone. I was to be on set and ready to go by 7am and it was being filmed out in the wilds somewhere. I was not comfortable with driving all that way in the early hours of the morning and immediately got on the phone and asked about train times. I found out even the proverbial milk train would be unable to get me there on time and the earliest I could expect to get there even with an additional taxi was 11am.

I rang him back in a blind panic. He shrugged off my worries and suggested I go up like **now** *and stay overnight. Now let's stop and think about this. Even had I rushed like a blue arsed fly, there was no way I would have been able to*

198

get there this side of midnight and I would then have had to walk the streets looking for a hotel with vacancies in the wee small hours in the middle of the summer season. I asked him for the production secretary's mobile phone number and gave her a call. I explained my problems and asked was there anyway I could be allowed to turn up at 11am. She answered with an emphatic 'NO'. She asked where I was coming from and I told her Nottingham. She was horrified and said she could not understand why I was coming all that way at that ungodly hour to do a job of work that could easily be done by a local agent using local actors. After all it was only a one day extra job!!! I was absolutely furious. I rang Reid back immediately but it went to answerphone and stayed on answerphone ever after.

This was where I naively expected Equity to come to my aid. I contacted them and they were inundated with complaints about this man and refused to help me. In my case I suppose I was lucky as there was just the matter of the £80 cost of the wig. A few weeks later a well known ventriloquist member told me he had recently been sent to a venue who knew nothing about his booking and Equity had taken that agent to court at enormous cost and got his £60 booking fee back. As in all walks of life, it seemed to me to be not what you know but who you know that really matters and on the strength of that story, I had paid my last Equity dues and as such gave up my treasurer's job.

Reid Graham did us all down and went to ground owing some of the members hundreds of pounds. There were other agents in the business too that come readily to mind who robbed us and members know only too well who I am speaking of. It speaks volumes that the most honest of them

all is still working today even though he is in his mid 80's.
That man is Jack Denman.

I missed the feeling of being useful though and on the back
of this exit from Equity; I joined my local parish council
where I have been ever since. I needed to feel that I was
contributing to life in some way and I have found I can do
this as a councillor. I recently found a photo where I am
doing that all important work and I have included it in the
book lest you think I wasted my time.

But right now auditioning for Cobblers in the mid 70's I
was a paid up although only a provisional Equity member
and no-one could question my right to be at that Bill
Maynard audition. I decided I would be more than 'ready', I
had the whole weekend to get word perfect, accordingly I
learned all my lines in the first episode off by heart, getting
my girls to help familiarise myself with them.
It opens with Bill asking his 'wife';
"Hello Betty midduck, ah'm starvin' what's fer me tea?"
I answer;
"Faggots duck."
The script was funny and my girls and I found ourselves
laughing out loud in places. It had obviously been written
specially for Bill Maynard.
Monday dawned and it was a fine sunny day as I recall. I
was blonde by this time and dressed carefully in a white
denim mini skirt (legs not *quite* so chunky now) and teamed
it with a white tee shirt. We had arranged to meet at the
venue - the Albany Hotel on Mount Street. I took the
escalator which ran virtually from the street and as it reached
the top, saw Jack and all the 'would be' cast sat around in the
reception area partaking of a tray of refreshments. I had been

too nervous to eat breakfast and had smoked at least a pack and a half of fags before I even got there.

Helping myself to tea and biscuits, I joined them on the smart leather sofas. I noticed for the first time, two young ladies sat apart and wondered if they were the actresses from London. After a few minutes wait a massive black ash double door opposite us partially opened and from the gloomy interior a female voice called out for Jack and he got up.
"Wish me luck" he said.
A disembodied hand reached out, took his elbow and drew him into the room. Half an hour later, Val Terry was called, then Charlie Bartle and finally me.

I had imagined the audition proper to be like others I had attended and would be conducted in a smallish room attended by perhaps Jack, the producer and myself. But when they finally did call my name, the reality was very different, scaringly different. The low ceilinged windowless room I was shown into was dimly lit and I supposed it to be a ballroom. Seated around the most enormous circular table littered with papers, coffee cups and overfull ash trays - proving they had obviously been sat there for some considerable time - were Howard Imber the writer who sat next to Bill Maynard, then Maynard Williams – Bill's real life son, a couple of Trent executives, ditto on a couple of young ladies whom I took to be secretaries, Jack, Val Terry and Charlie Bartle. No pressure there then!

Bill said hello and introduced me to the others. He told them I was reading for the part of Beryl his 'wife'. Terse and and to the point he dived straight in and caught me completely off my balance as he said;
"Hello Betty midduck, ah'm starvin', what's fer me tea?"
Instinctively I replied

"Faggots duck."

"Awww, not blumming faggots again. We 'ad blummin faggots yesterday an' we 'ad 'em the day before annall, ah'm just about sick of blummin' faggots. Can't we ev summat else?"

"I'd love to cook yer summat different duck but 'ow can I when ya spend all our money on seducing that pop group o' yourn."

There was a ripple of laughter.

(I instantly broke out in a cold sweat. Subsidising you prat! SUBSIDISING! I admonished myself, sure I had blown it.)

"Sorry, subsidising. I..I am a bit nervous." I apologised.

Bill turned to the writer who was the living image of John Junkin and said;

"Leave that in Howard, I like it."

Howard scribbled something on his script.

"No cause to be nervous here lovey, we are all pissing in the same pot. But leave the jokes to me eh?"

Bill said his voice now warm and welcoming. It was the first time I had ever heard that expression 'pissing in the same pot'.

We continued to read the entire first episode, each of us taking our cues from Bill. After my initial faux pas I settled down and was word perfect for the rest of the read through. He then asked us to excuse him and to wait outside and he would join us shortly. The two ladies, who had been patiently sat in reception all this time, were now called and Jack said he too thought they were the actresses sent by the big guns from London. *Convinced I had blown it I castigated myself for my stupidity. 'I bet they won't make a balls up of it', I thought enviously as they passed me.* Minutes later the door opened and the two ladies came out followed moments later by Bill and his cohorts who emerged in a light hearted bantering mood as the two girls headed for the escalator.

"Congratulations all of you and welcome on board," Bill boomed, "Let's go round the corner to the Playhouse bar and christen the show."

Despite my gaff, I had got the part, we had *all* got the part. We had something to celebrate. Sat in the bar was a familiar face and the face winked at me. It was Maurice Kaufman (He was a well known actor and was divorced from no ess a woman than Honor Blackman.) He seemed to know Bill and came over and joined us. I was gobsmacked!

It was the beginning of an exciting six weeks. I not only played the wife part, but also a giddy young girl at a party and other bits and bob's too as did we all. It was recorded before a live audience and lots of my family, neighbours and friends came to the improvised studio at the Albany to support me and be a part of it. On the last night of recording Radio Trent threw a celebratory party to which we were all invited. Bill said he was considering televising Cobblers and wanted me to be in it too. I thought not and told him so.

"Who are you kidding? With comedy actresses like Yootha Joyce, June Whitfield and Barbara Windsor available, you are not going to pick me."

"Oh yes I am," he said, narrowing his eyes in that way he does and tapping the side of his nose knowingly,

"...because you would do it for nothing to get your foot in the door and that would leave more money for me."

He was quite right of course but it never came to fruition so I was unable to put his words to the test.

But on the strength of that series, my expensive and at that time prestigious Just owning an Equity card gave me kudos and added another spoke to my wheel. I did a couple of marriage guidance video's, went to London several times and did voice overs for the Sun newspaper, an advert for 'Loot' the 'buy and sell' newspaper, BBC programme ads and various other things for radio advertising and I also did a lot of extra work for the Fremantle the Australian Media company that makes Neighbours.

In one film, the name of which escapes me, done for them at East Midlands airport, we had a huge scene to do amid hundreds of curious travellers so it was fraught with difficulty from the off.

"Annnnd...ACTION...."

Little Johnny excitedly rushed up to the main actor Michael Attwell and nearly tripped him up.

"Wee gooin' on aeroplane...."

The actor grinned and bent down from his great height to ruffle his hair.

"CUT AND RESET."

"Annd ACTION."

Robert Kilroy Silk had just arrived to catch a flight and unknowingly walked straight across scene!

"CUT AND RESET."

"Annnd ACTION"

The unmistakable Sir Ian Botham had alighted from an inner city flight and walked ram rod straight across the set to get to the Hertz office to pick up his rental car. You couldn't legislate for this!

"CUT AND RESET."

Jack trusted me and pushed me forward every chance he got. I got a part in a training video for the marriage guidance and thought it rich as my own marriage crumbled beneath me. There was only one job out of the many he got me that I ever turned down; It was to play a bit part as an artistes model. I simply had to sit there stark naked in a studio whilst the play action went on around me as the artist painted. It was worth a massive £2.000! I could have judicious use of a towel I was told, but there were no sizes to comfort me and I thought it might well be a face flannel rather than the bath sheet I really wanted! I thought of my kids and the reaction they would be bound to get at school the next day, the chants of 'I saw your mum on the telly last night, she had no clothes on!' I could not do it to them and turned it down preferring to keep my 'bits' private!

I was given another few lines in the Anglo American production of Signs and Wonders starring; James Earl Jones, Donald Pleasence, Prunella Scales, Collin Farrell and David Warner. It is essentially the story of a charlatan who claims he can 'heal by touch'. In the scene I was in I played the mother of a young boy prone to epileptic fits who, before a large fanatical gathering, has his head touched to heal him. It has the opposite effect and the lad collapses on the floor in a heap. I race to my 'son's' side and scream at the man asking him what he has done to him. This was all filmed literally just around the corner where my sister Sandra had a pub in Riddings in Derbyshire.

But Stuart Burge (yes I wondered who he was at the time too) of 'Sons and Lovers' fame (aha!) was about to come into my life again.

"Joy? Jack Denman dear."

"Hi jack, what can I do for you?"

"Stop hi-jacking me for a start, I have too much work to do! You can check your diary for the 5th." I looked at my huge planner pinned onto the wall in front of me. It was free.

"It's free Jack."

"I have just had Stuart Burge on the phone."

"Who's Stuart Burge?" I queried.

"'This bleedin' table's been laid more times than me...' Stuart Burge?"

"Oh THAT Stuart Burge." I giggled.

"Yes, *that* Stuart Burge. He is looking for someone with a local accent to play the midwife in The Rainbow. Its only a days extra work but he has asked specifically for you."

"Wow."

I don't impress easily, I was impressed.

"Book it in, it's Friday the 17th at 12 noon. I'll give you more details as soon as I get them."

The production centre was in a church hall and I went straight there upon my arrival. Everyone was at lunch so I sat in the quiet of the hall and read my paper. At 2pm on the dot, I was directed to the make-up wardrobe caravans. The head make up artiste shook his head wondering what on earth he was supposed to do with me. I was listed as a dumpy typical village harridan come to deliver a baby. I had naturally glamoured myself up with long blonde tresses and wore a smart cream trench coat, cream boots and a matching oh so *expensive* cream satin scarf decorated with tiny black dots which I remember with painful regret, as I accidentally left it behind and despite my many enquiries it was never found.

He sat me in front of a mirror, stood behind me and pondered what he could do with my hair. I pulled off my wig, yanked at the hair pins and down tumbled my long fine dark brown hair. He was ecstatic. He wound it up into a bun, pulled a few wisps down, sprayed it grey and further whitened the temples. Wardrobe clothed me in a long drab brown dress with a sackcloth pinny, added a bit of padding here and there and bingo I was done. The effect was amazing. I barely recognised myself.

Ready as I would ever be, I was then taken to the venue which turned out to be a street in Cossall. It was amazing what they had done with the house they had chosen to film in. Cossall is the sort of essentially typical English village everyone wants to live in. The street whereon we filmed was smart and well cared for...excepting for that one house that had been dressed for its D H Lawrence part. Bathed in warm spring sunshine, it looked like a Victorian picture postcard. The walls had been dressed down to look 'sootified' and the interior was furnished with heavy oak furniture of the most primitive kind.

A fireplace of the Moffat Street variety had been installed and even held glowing red coals that warmed the room. On closer inspection however I found the glowing coals to be a couple of red electric bulbs set among the cobbles. The walls were dressed with gloomy faded wallpaper and portraits of sombre faced, straight laced supposed relatives took pride of recess place either side of the fireplace. But it was upstairs where I was to work that really stood out.

They had actually removed all the inner walls thereby creating a giant loft. Sat uncomfortably in the corner was the editor who watched what was being produced on a screen as it happened. He was uncomfortable because he was sat on the toilet that had been incongruously left when the walls had been removed. Stuart greeted me and asked was I really that elegant lady who had walked in a bare hour ago? Oh those make up and wardrobe staff are brilliant.

He took me through my paces, gave me a few words to say and we went for a trial shot. I had to clump clumsily upstairs carrying and spilling a heavy pitcher of water, watched by the other Brangwen children. Then go into the only bedroom with a door and shut it behind me. From behind the door I was recorded making various noises associated with the delivery of a baby. 'Come on now gel, nearly there, just a tad more effort...should be like shelling pea's the number yo've ad.' etc. Throughout there was a bit of screeching and grunting from the 'mother' and the inevitable weak cry of a new born baby. I then had to emerge from the room, walk past the huge double bed that had all the children huddled together in it, went to the top of the stairs and called

"It's a lad Mester Brangwen, yer've gorra 'nother little lad."

Then footsteps clattering on a wooden staircase are heard as Tom Bell presumably tears up to see his latest child. I turn on my heel again passing the children who ask in an excited cacophony of voices 'can we see him' 'can we hold him nurse' 'bring him out to show us' and 'is me mam alright?' and I smile at them and return to my patient and that was it. Technically there was just a small query as to how loud I was to shout downstairs but Stuart seemed happy with the sound level and we went for it. After only two takes, he thanked me and said it was a wrap for me. I was back home again just after three in time to greet my kids from school. A nice little £40 earner.

That same night I had a call from Jack to say Stuart had called him and was so pleased with what I had done, he was 'making me up'. This means that I was to be put on a walk on 1 fee. Then, a few weeks later, Jack called me again.

"Joy, Jack here dear. I have just had a cheque from The Rainbow for you and they have made an error. You know Stuart said he was making you up? Well he has but for some reason the finance department have taken the cost of a day's extra pay out of it and so its short."

Ever mindful of stamp costs and how best to save money, I replied

"That's ok Jack hold on to the cheque they've sent and as soon as they send the remainder, pop them both in together and it'll save you a bit of postage."

There was an unusual silence and then he said;

"You are a funny sod Joy James, anyone else would have asked how much the cheque was for, but not you."

Now I was curious.

"How much is it for?"

"£100 from the BBC1 showing on Saturday night and a guaranteed £100 for the BBC2 repeat show the night after, ergo, the cheque is for £200 not the forty you have been expecting.....aanndd...he has put your name in the credits!"

My heart nearly stopped with the shock.

Let me tell you, it is one thing to see your face on the TV, its quite another to see your name roll up in the credits...fast forward, slow down MIDWIFE~ ~ ~ JOY JAMES....rewind, fast forward, slow down... MIDWIFE ~ ~ ~JOY JAMES...rewind....

Lord only knows what I would have done if I had ever made anything like top billing! Nice work if you can get it and for once I got it albeit on a small scale. To this day I still get a yearly cheque from that job, albeit it only a few pence these days.

And if that was the best paid job – and for me it was – there was one job that was conversely both the best and worst job of all, The Token King by Ray Kilby. The best part was playing Samantha Morton's mother in her first ever film and the worst part was getting paid the princely sum of nothing for doing it, not even expenses! We were told that it was to be an entry into some sort of film festival and as such had virtually no budget, so pay was out. The Token King is a wonderful little film. It got shown on Channel Four at least twice and I have my own copy and even that I had to pay £10 for. It was a nice production to be involved with though and I felt privileged to be working with some great folk. At that time Samantha Morton was a teenager barely in the business and it was obvious even then what an amazingly talented girl she was. She had no airs and graces but was so good an actress in her part. I told her she was destined to go far; she had that certain Je nous se qua, something you can't buy in bottles. Within a year I was proved right as she was working for the Disney Corporation!

CHAPTER SEVENTEEN

THE PRICE WAS ALWAYS RIGHT.

I had worked with Leslie Crowther on a few occasions and apart from us both coming from the same neck of the woods, give or take a thousand times difference in the way we were bought up, we Nottingham folk kind of cleaved together. I well remember our first meeting. I was doing a freebie at the Post Office club on Derby Road and was actually singing on stage when as guest of honour at this charity night, he walked in. I had the audience eating out of my hand but their attention was lost when the door opened and a ripple of 'he's here' went round the room. I stopped singing.

"Yes folks, the man you have come to see has arrived."

All eyes watched him as, not wanting to intrude on my work; he hurriedly and smilingly took his seat.

"Let's give a big round of applause ladies and gentlemen to your guest for the evening, Mr Harry Worth!"

He had a ciggie in his mouth as I said it and he laughed through it and blew hot tobacco and ash all over the table and just had the empty cigarette paper tube stuck to his lips. It was really funny. He was a smashing bloke and I am sure many of you are nodding your heads in silent agreement. He never acquired that 'edge' that affects some folk to their detriment when dealing with others. It's quite common and is called being a big head. Not so Leslie. He was a charming man.

A new show was being tried out at Central. It was a U.S idea that had taken their viewers by storm and was now under the management of William G Stewart (G for Gladstone...not a lot of people know that!) It was The Price is Right and was in its early stages here. In its rehearsal days it needed actors to play the part of audience members and we were required to respond enthusiastically by screaming, shouting and waving about of arms when the host called out JIM SMITH, COME ON DOWN! It was to be a once weekly, two shows a day job that would provide steady work for four continuous weeks and paid enough to take my family on a caravan holiday each year.

The first few dummy run shows we did featured different hosts. I remember doing a trial show with Joe Brown but it was the genuine and undoubted charm of Leslie Crowther that finally won the day and the much coveted job. He was smooth, unflappable and utterly professional. It was on the strength of that job that he moved from his huge house in London and bought an even bigger one in Bath. Proud as punch he would regularly bring me photos of how the refurbishment was coming and carried a little white plastic wallet full of shots of the house and grounds. He took a keen interest in us as people too and knew every one of us by our first names. I remember he always came and sat with us in the canteen at central and many a lunch hour was spent choking on our food as he cracked gag after gag.
"There w's this bloke..." off he would go; his Nottingham twang had long since had the vowels manicured but in the joke telling he slipped effortlessly back into the twang.
"and he pulls up on this 'ere pub car park in his battered owd Ford Cortina, at the same time as a brand new Mercedes. He was gob smacked when he saw who was driving it. It were

Billy Smith the class clahn; the kid voted 'The least likely to succeed.'

"Billy lad, how yer doin' mi owd mucker?"

"Not as well as yo' bi't looks on it, that's some car."

"Ay it's not bad but worra bout yo'? Yo' were't class brainbox?"

"Yeah wan't ah? After leavin' school I went onto Uni', took me masters then did a couple of year at business school. In the late 60's I founded me own company selling bonds, stocks and shares and then it all crashed in the 70's and I lost the lot. I see yo've done well for yerrsen entcha?"

"Yeah, I have actually. As ya know, I left school with no qualifications and went straight on the dole. I were a sod and would spend the dole money on booze and then be in purgatory waiting for me next cheque. One morning I woke and desperately needed a drink. I looked in my pocket and all I had left was £2. It would just about buy me a pint. I started off down to the pub but on the way had to pass a timber yard and out front on the pavement was a huge pile of lumber with a price tag of £2.

Summat in me snapped and I suddenly saw what I could do with that wood. I bought it and set to work, spendin' a couple of days sawin' and hammerin' and finally shaped it into a tidy shed. The bloke next door saw it and offered me £100 for it. I set off for the pub to celebrate, got as far as the wood yard and spent the money on red cedar instead. Again it took me a couple of day's hard graft but I persevered and made an even bigger and better model which sold for £400. I realised I had found me bent and the next lot of wood I got was the finest pale oak yo've ever seen. I did a shed with double glazed windows, power sockets and even phone points. It was tremendous. Then I won eight million quid on the lottery and I thought 'sod these sheds...'!'"

Bobby Charles was a regular on this show as was I. A lot of the lads who did it vied with each other to keep the rehearsals fresh by being the most original in their answers to Leslie's questions and many was the time the place fell about when Leslie called out one of their names.

"BOBBY CHARLES, COME ON DOWN..."
'Applause' read the board held up to us by the floor manager....we dozen or so pretenders 'applaused' wildly trying to emulate 3oo audience members as Bobby ran down the stairs to join Leslie.....

"Welcome to contestants row on The Price is Right Bobby, now tell me a bit about yourself...What is your job?"
"I am a pox doctor!"

And this was said with the very straightest of faces but Leslie could not hold it and collapsed to his knees in hysterics as did the rest of the staff with the exception of the all important director William G Stewart who took it very seriously. Slowly the laughter would die down and on went the show.

"CHARLIE BARTLE COME ON DOWN....and what do you do for a living?
"I am a patient of the last contestant!" he said with a twinkle in his aged eye! He was in his 80's then! William G made an exception for Charlie and roared with laughter along with the rest of us.

Oh how we LOVED doing this work and the additional bonus was, we got paid for it too

Charlie was a comedian who dressed as a drunken tramp and used his little Yorkshire terrier in his act. He would stumble on stage with a glass in his hand (he didn't drink) and the dog in the deep pocket of his black ragged overcoat.

214

He would begin by telling the audience that this dog was trained to obey him instantly. He would then take the dog out of his pocket, put him on the floor and order him to STAY! This was the signal for the dog to lope off looking over his shoulder and make for the dressing room. Once there, the dog would settle down and wait for his master. The audience lapped it up. He was what was known as a clean comic. Not only did he never use a bad swear word on stage, he never told a mucky joke either.

His favourite gag was;

A blind man and his dog were out for a walk one day and as they got to the pedestrian crossing the dog obediently stopped. Whilst they waited the dog cocked his leg up and peed all over the man trousers and shoes. The man shook his leg and then fumbled in his pocket, bought out a dog biscuit and gave it to him. A man stood watching and said

"I have never known such kindness in my whole life."

"What do you mean?" asked the man.

"Well the dog's peed all over you and you give him a biscuit."

"That's not kind; I am just trying to find out where his mouth is so I can kick him up the arse!"

He was one of the drivers that had never needed to take a test and his driving left much to be desired. I went with him once on an audition and the journey was a fast nightmare. When we got to the venue as he merely parked the car he hit three others. He drove fast and furious and when I finally got home, my feet ached from subconsciously putting the brakes on for the whole of the journey. One night, returning from a whist drive in Bingham Nottingham, both he and his dog were killed in a car accident on the bye-pass.

In late 88 early 89 the press blazed the story that Leslie Crowther like his father before him, was an alcoholic and he was booked into a clinic for treatment. His honesty about his condition was only what we expected of him. I think people in Nottingham who knew him personally were shocked because in all the years I had known him, I had never seen him take an alcoholic drink and whilst working as a contestant on The Price Is Right, I had stood up close and personal to him and had never even got a whiff of booze, he being nothing if not totally professional. He went on to beat the drink and never touched it again. Then he had that appalling accident. He was matter of factly breathalysed but it was clear. To lose him in this way, coincidentally the same way his father died, was hard to take. He was a much loved and well respected man.

Another job I was to go on and do was Hardwicke House, a show about teenagers in secondary school and it was seen as a follow on to the Please Sir! series, only with sex. I turned up alongside many others and was immediately taken to one side and given the job of an irate parent. I had to barge into the headmaster's office and take him to task about something he had said to my child. He would mumble an ineffective excuse and I was to lose my rag and do him physical harm. On 'action' I charged through the door, screaming at him, grabbed him by the scruff of the neck and bent him backwards over his desk. This was being filmed from outside the classroom so no clear words could be heard but I heard a peal of laughter and on the retake, they moved the camera and it now caught the shot that looked at though I was doing something entirely different to him.

They had made me up to walk on one and I waited anxiously for that episode. But the public were outraged at the interactive sexual actions of the kids and teachers in the pilot show and it was unceremoniously axed and has never seen the light of day since!

The Life and Loves of a She Devil (1986) was another BBC production I was lucky enough to get on. It was filmed in a private house in Smalley Derbyshire. The house was simply stunning and had a huge hall to die for. It was unusual in that all the interior walls were rounded with no corners to speak of. It had an indoor swimming pool that had a roof that could open up like a convertible car and a kitchen that would pass envious muster even unto today all these years later. The bedrooms had unheard of in those days, dressing rooms attached and the furnishings were sumptuous.

To get to it, you drove down a really rather ordinary street, turned left into what looked to be a simple track between two houses and there at the bottom of a slight hill was this unbelievable mansion of a place set in its own huge grounds. (I believe it was built for a man who sold the then innovative plastic food bags!) This was the 'clinic' where Julie T Wallace turned herself into a mirror image of her lover (Dennis Waterman's) wife played by Patricia Hodge. Miss Wallace had to have huge amounts of padding to depict her as a grossly over weight woman and there were various body suits hanging around the corridors like those of the Bubbles DeVere variety worn by Matt Lucas in Little Britain that she had to wear and they were so lifelike but totally weird.

I arrived at the 'clinic' at 7am, got taken into wardrobe and make-up and was set upon by these imaginative girls who could turn a sow into a princess. They 'glammed' me up and approved the electric blue silk dress I had bought with me and the whacking high heeled shoes. The part I had was the first shot of the day and saw me arriving at the face lift clinic in a big Yankee car. The car pulls up, I swing out of my seat and sashay my way into the foyer.... 'aaand cut'!

We practised this a few times whilst they got the car speed and camera angles just right and we got *our* timing spot on before we went for a 'take'. I find myself counting my way through this sort of work. I think it helps to pace it better. Roll down the gravel drive...two...three...four...stop.... open door....one....two...swing right out of the car and sashay into the foyer saying something to 'Kingston' my driver husband. 'aaand cut!' 'Reset'.... We did it about three times before they were happy and began to move on. It was at this point someone gave a squeal and pointed at my chest. As I had swung out of the car, my dress had twisted and was now stuck fast behind my right bosom showing a wide expanse of white Wonderbra! And despite their insistence on continuity no-one even noticed. In another scene, it opens on a party in the clinic and in the opening shot the camera zooms in on a large pair of bosoms popping out of a black skin tight cat suit. Them's mine!!!!!

Another job I did was in Nanny a series set during the war with Wendy Craig. This was the exact opposite of the previous glamorous role. I played a chaperone bringing a bus load of evacuated London youngsters into Nanny's village. This was filmed in Lincolnshire in the unbearable heat of high summer but the scene was set later in the year and I was dressed for it in a thick heavy tweed coat, tea coloured lisle stockings, forties styled wig and an appalling hat! They bought in bags of dried leaves and scattered them along the country lane down which we interminably travelled with the kids take after take after take.

Now I'll let you into a secret and explain about those wigs. It was always a mystery to me as to how the likes of (say) Dick Emery could wear a wig on TV and turn himself into woman without us seeing the join. But it was on such productions as this that I found out the answer and it was amazingly simple really. The wigs have a small inch wide white net all round the edge that comes into contact with the forehead and temples. This is glued on with spirit gum! It feels uncomfortable, looks silly up close and personal but cannot be detected by the camera.

The next scene calls for us to 'arrive' and meet Nanny and the 'would be' caretaker parents. Our destination was a field in the middle of nowhere. All around us the farmers were gathering in their sheaths....and disturbing zillions of tiny midges which descended on us like a black cloud. They drove us all crazy and wormed their way into our mouths and eyes, under the netting of my wig and wriggled non stop trying to escape their sticky end. They further settled onto my chest and squirmed their way into my cleavage. Ugh!

It got so bad we couldn't work and they called a halt whilst one of the crew raced into Lincoln city and bought back dozens of anti insect sprays and gave us each one. I gratefully sprayed my face and chest with its cooling vapour but the damn things stuck to the moisture and made it even worse. When I finally got home that night and stripped off to jump into a nice cool desperately needed shower, I found about a million of them in the bottom of my bra and in other private places that frankly they had no business going into!

CHAPTER EIGHTEEN

JOY JAMES CAN'T SPEAK THE LINGO!

In the early 90's John Harvey's 'Resnick' was adapted for TV and I auditioned for, got and played the part of a barmaid in one episode. It was filmed in the Peacock on Mansfield road and was a simple scene requiring me to come and ask Resnick (Tom Wilkinson – remember his hilarious role as he taught the lads how to dance in the stripping scene in The Full Monty? That scene in the dole office queue as they all subconsciously go through the dance movements to the sound of a radio playing in the background still gets me chuckling after all these years!) The scene was simple; he comes in asking about food and it went something like this;

Me; "Ayyup duck, what can ah get ya?"

Him; "What do you have to eat?"

Me; "Ohh," I look at my watch, "yo've left it a bit late duck? All we got left is sandwiches."

Him; "What sort of sandwiches?"

Me; "Cheese? Cheese n onion?" I pause a beat, "Onion?"

That episode was shown whilst I was actually abroad on holiday and when I got back I was stopped in Netherfield as I shopped and told that I had been criticised in the Nottingham Evening Post letters page for the false accent I had used in Resnick! I was able to get a copy of the paper and read what the writer, a Mr Billiald had said. It was something on the lines of 'once again the inevitable plastic accented 'ayyup duck' has been used to portray the difficult Nottingham accent.' He went on to say I did not sound at all realistic! Me gob as they say, was well and truly smacked! I picked up my pen, proving on this occasion it really was mightier than the sword and wrote:

"Ah'm norr 'appy! Ah understand from reading yore letters page that thi's bin a bit a bother abaut the Nottingham accent used in the new BBC production o' Resnick. Nah ah'm gerrin' on me 'igh bobbo a bit 'ere ah know, burr ah understand as 'ow one o' yore writers, a Mester Billiald 'as said 'as 'ow the only person to come close wus that Peacock waitress, and she was described as 'avin' said in a plastic accent "Ayyup duck."

Ah do admit as thi's bin a lot o' bad examples o' this difficult an' ugly dialect, but would Mester Billiald explain just worr is a Nottingham accent if that want? Ah do confess as ah've gorr a vested interest in 'is reply, on'y ah 'appen ter know that gel as played the waitress an' ah know as she's lived in Nottingham all 'er bleddy life, an' 'Ayyup duck' is still the customary greetin' o' the more common folk.

Thi's times when ah 'ere that gel talk an' ah think as 'ow she'll never gerr another part wi' such a board vocal delivereh. In fact if truth be known the on'y wok she's ever 'ad ''as bin by virtue of 'er 'evvin' a broad accent.

Nah, 'ow do ah know tharr accent was authentic? Frum the age o' three, that gel wus dragged up in St Ann's ('er mam used ter sell tuffee apples off 'er front doorstep on Moffat street) she went ter the threp'nny rush at the Cavo ev'ry Sat'dey, 'ad 'er clowes frum Jaceh Pownalls, went ter Bluebell 'ill an' Pierrepont schools, wokked at Jersey Kapwood's an' gorr 'er fust marital 'ome in 'yson Green, so ah reckon as 'ow she's gorra be a bit of 'n expert in the lingo. An' if tharr int enough ter prove me point, ah shoulda thought yo'd a guessed by nah Mester Billiald, norr on'y do ah know that Peacock waitress, ah AM that Peacock waitress.

Listen 'ere...

AH'M norr 'appy! Ah understand frum readin' yore letters page that thi's bin a bit a bother abaut the Nottingham accent used in the new BBC production o' *Resnick*.

Nah, ah'm gerrin on me 'igh bobbo a bit 'ere ah know, burr ah understand as 'ow one o' yore writers, a Mester Billiald, has said as 'ow the only person that cum close wus that Peacock waitress, an she wus described as 'avin said, in plastic accent: "Ayup duck" [Opinion, April 8].

Ah do admit as thi's bin a lot o' bad examples o' this difficult an' ugly dialect, but would Mester Billiald explain just warr is a Nottingham accent if that want? Ah do confess ah've gorr a vested interest in 'is reply, on'y ah 'appen ter know that gel as played the waitress an' ah know as she's lived in Nottingham all 'er bleddy life, an 'ayup duck is still the customary greetin' o' the more common folk.

Thi's times when ah 'ear that gel talk an' ah think to messen as 'ow she'll never gerr another part wi' such a broad vocal delivereh. In fact, if the truth were known, the on'y wok she's ever 'ad 'as bin by virtue of 'er evvin' a broad accent!

PRIZE LETTER

This week's winning letter — first published on Wednesday — is from Joy James of Colwick Park Close, Old Colwick. She wins a classic Waterman fountain pen worth £15 and is now a contender for our monthly Golden Pen award

Nah, 'ow do ah know tharr accent was authentic? Frum the age o' three, that gel was dragged up in St Ann's ('er mam used ter sell tuffee apples off 'er front doorstep on Moffatt Street) she went ter threp'nny rush at the Cavo ev'ry Sat'dey, 'ad 'er clowes frum Jaceh Pownalls, went ter Bluebell 'ill, Pierrepont an' John Player schools, wokked at Jersch Kapwood's an' gorr 'er fust marital 'ome in a backstreet terrace in 'yson Green, so ah reckon as 'ow she's gorra be a bit of 'n expert in the lingo.

An' if tharr int enough ter prove me point, ah shoulda thought yo'd a guessed by nah, Mester Billiald, norr on'y do ah know that Peacock waitress, ah AM that Peacock waitress!

LOCAL LINGO MADE ME GRIN

I FEEL that as I write this I still have a silly grin on my face from reading Joy James' "Ah'm norr 'appy" letter in tonight's *Evening Post* [April 15].

I read through it twice and then had a go at reading it out loud to try and capture that unusual Nottingham dialect. Very funny, I thought.

During the early war years I had a girlfriend who lived and, I feel sure, was born in the Meadows. We both worked at Boots, Island Street. Although she basically spoke quite good English she could at the drop of a hat lapse in "Nottinghamese" or is it "Meadowese" (I wonder if the Meadows dialect differs from St Ann's?)

Some of the Boots firemen were a bit cheeky and if she was the recipient of what one might describe as a "knowing look" as she went through the London Road gates on the way home, she would most likely, with hands on hips, say: "What y' gozzing at y' gozzy force-bob yo?"

I think I would translate that as "why are you looking at me like that you forceful, too familar person!"

Perhaps Joy James could do a better translation? I will finish by saying ayup m'duck Joy, gi us some more Nottinghamese.

DENNIS BROOKS
Shelford Crescent,
Burton Joyce.

Talk of the town

I AM 81 years old and when I read the letter from Joy Jones about our Nottingham slang I thought: We were never taught to write like that!

I still say Ey up duck and In it?, Ain it? and War it? — most of the old Radford lot did.

I have a grandson and he was born in Lancs. He came to stop with me for a week and one of the ladies who lived against me said to him "Ello duck" and he turned round and said: "I'm not a duck, I'm a love". That's what they call them up there.

Give me the good old days, anytime. We enjoyed ourselves then.

B. GARNER (Mrs)
Falston Road,
Beechdale Estate.

Language we loved

ABOUT the Nottingham accent:

Ooo, Joy James — ah luv ya. Ya the ony one av ever known oo can purrit daun on paper. Burr it's norr ugleh, it's luvleh!

IRENE FRYER
Elms Park,
Ruddington.

As you can see from the cuttings above, my letter generated a fair bit of correspondence some of which I have included. A few days later there was a knock on my door and a Mr and Mrs Billiald came to call. I invited them in for a mashin' o'

222

tea and we 'ed a good natter! Can't do the accent? Gerrautonnit! Ohh that seems such a long time ago....but the odd thing is, I won the Letter of the Month award and with it a Waterman's pen with an eighteen carat gold nib, worth reputedly £300. I still have it.

This show went on to have a premier in a London theatre and I got an invite. A lady friend of mine Barbara .....very kindly took me there in her Mercedes and we had a nice evening.

They say you can't be happy all the time but these really were my salad days and I was utterly happy and content. I had a good home life, loved my job and frequently entertained our friends and colleagues at home. I discovered that I could decorate and put my new found talent to good use, wall papering and painting my home turning it into a smart and welcoming place to live and visit. Gradually I began to work on my garden. Previously the garden was nothing more than a meadow with a pond resembling a puddle, but now I turned my attention to it and had a proper turf lawn put down. One weekend, a friend and his wife came to visit. He remarked how nice the garden was beginning to look and I said that much as I enjoyed the puddle like pond I was either going to have to have it made bigger or it was going to be filled in. He told me to get him a few beers in, take his wife out of his hair and he would do it. When I got back it was three times the original size and I love it.

In the picture you can see below there is, standing guard over the pond, a six foot tall heron. This is a piece of art carved out of one solid tree, the bark being left on to effectively represent the birds feathers. You will find it hard to believe but I got that from the Colwick car boot sale for the princely sum of £20 having talked the owner down from £120 and at that, they delivered it! It absolutely weighs a ton and when I went to site him, he fell and his beak just about cracked my skull open. OUCH! I forgave him, he is worth it.

But what with him and the netting tacked over the pond, I manage to keep the herons away from making a meal as they all too often have, of my beloved koi carp and gold pond fish. This garden is my pride and joy. It's got its fair share of weeds, but like the dust in my lounge, I don't notice them. Apart from the occasional weeding of the pebbled areas, I simply mow the lawn and strim the edges to keep it looking as nice as I want it to look. I don't make hard work of it, I just enjoy it. But no-one has ever come in to it and not said what a lovely garden it is.

A couple of times a year the fish spawn and I put in a piece of cotton wool to catch the eggs. I then fetch them indoors and daily watch them grow inside their eggs through a magnifying glass until they hatch. It's such a joyful thing to watch. They are half the length and thickness of an eyelash to begin with but they grow rapidly and there are a dozen about three weeks old on my kitchen window ledge even as I write.

Its strikes me as odd that they all begin the same size and yet there is always one who will outgrow the others. Last year, one (I christened him the Incredible Hulk) grew so big so fast I didn't know what to make of him or why the huge growth spurt....until I saw him swimming around with the still wriggling tail of one of his 'brothers' sticking out of his mouth. I scooped him up in a tea strainer and put him into the pond proper and asked him how he liked it!

My grandson Sam in my garden.

I recently met up with a long lost friend and she remembers all the lovely parties I used to do for family birthdays and Christmas. It was on the day of one of these dinner parties that my kids presented me with a tougher than usual challenge. You know how they have a habit of dropping something on you at a moments notice? I was frantically busy in the kitchen preparing the food for the evening as well as dealing with a delivery of a birthday cake, the man from the pub knocked on the front door wanting to know where to put the barrel of beer he had bought (I very nearly told him!) and my two youngest raced in through the back door and asked could they enter a fancy dress party?

"Oh of course you can," I answered wondering if I should put th candles on the cake now, or leave it until a bit nearer the time.

"What can I go as?" Cindy asked.

"Anything you want, I'm sure I can make you something."

"You won't have time!"

"Of course I'll have time, when is it?"

"Now!"

"What do you mean '**now**'?"

"They are doing it right now and we want to enter."

I had shooed them out earlier with their friends to spend their pocket money on the village fete and gala. For a second or two I was so flummoxed I was tempted to say no, but I quickly grabbed Cindy and turned her into a passable Hilda Ogden (ask ya mam!) Then I turned to Zoe. She was going to be a much bigger problem. I suppose she would be about 3 or 4 and she had obviously had a lot of fun with candy floss at the gala for her hands and face were sticky and filthy. Quick as a flash I realised it would be quicker to blacken her face and arms some more, hide her blonde hair under a woolly winter hat I owned, thus turning her into a Golliwog doll. They raced off back to the gala in high spirits and won!

On the home front my kids were doing really well in school. They attended what I consider the best school I have ever known, St John the Baptist in Colwick. I remember the teachers with real affection and gratitude; Mr Brown the headmaster, Miss Salt, Mrs Squires, Miss Custerson. Here real values were instilled into mine and my neighbours children by these dedicated staff; Barbara's kids, Penny, Steven and Gay; my next door but one neighbours Geoff and

Marion Moor's kids Kerry and Brent; Lyn's kids Peter, Caroline and Suzy; from across the road, Bob and Vera's daughter Joanne Creates – her of the fiery red hair; Natalie and Danny Waterall next door; the Hutton clan Jimmy and Donna; Mick and Bobby Cooper's kids twins Katy and Emily and their siblings Sally and James and I watched with pride as they all grew and flourished in this small healthy community. It was an absolute joy to watch them grow and to be part of their lives. As parents we couldn't have done so badly because not one of the above mentioned kids went wrong, all of them turning into fine upstanding citizens to be proud of.

My Laura, an out and out Tomboy, was and is still in the same hurry she'd been from the day she was born. She rushed headlong into adolescence totally unprepared for it. How well I recall her first ever real date. It was with Jimmy Hutton, she'd be about 14 at the time and was in a fever of excitement, seemingly spending the entire day getting ready much to our amusement. She was finally all done and dusted and presented herself to us for approval. I can see her now; she was wearing a new 1970's fashionable denim blue corduroy trouser suit with shocking pink sequinned flower trim.

She looked lovely; poised, sophisticated and well groomed. Her hair was quite long, still with that inbuilt kink she had been born with and it had evidently taken a while to get rid of this curl she so hated. She had that glowing enviable skin that only very young girls seem to have and to put make-up on top of it really was guilding the lily, but she'd slapped a bit on anyway. We told her how nice she looked and meant it and off she went. Once out of the door, she did her usual and ran as if the very devil himself was after her and by the time she got to the top of the drive, her sophistication had vanished and so had her careful grooming!

Cindy meanwhile was the exact opposite. She was calm sweet and considerate and being very feminine sailed effortlessly into puberty, but with a crafty bent! Whilst Laura would lie through her teeth to get out of trouble (and don't we all?) Cindy could not lie, but she could tell the truth in such a way that kept her out of trouble. I came home once from a long haul nights work to find a note on my pillow which read;

Mum, I have done something really silly. I have tried to cut my hair and made a horrible bad mess of it. I know you will be very angry with me and I am so sorry, but please don't shout at me and try to remember you were a kid yourself once and you must have done silly things too.

How could any mum be angry? Like I said, she was crafty but clever with it.

There were occasions when I took my kids with me on (say) TV work for which they got paid – Zoe did quite a lot of it and one time was offered a chance to get into Central workshop a TV acting school but she turned it down flat and has never regretted it. Once she was offered the chance to audition as the helicopter link for Central TV's weather eye and she turned that down too. On one occasion I was doing a charity working very locally and took little Zoe with me, she'd be about five. I sprang out on the stage, picked up the mike and began to sing. I got to the end of the song and then addressed the audience and started a little banter with them. A small voice interrupted me shouting;

"Don't talk mummy, sing!"

From my days of living in Clifton I had still kept links with its social club and sang quite a few times at their charity do's. These were organised by a man known only to me as Scots John. He had a passion for Blesma (British Limbless Ex Service Men's Association) and got me involved in his fund raising. Their Blackpool based home was his special pet project and he worked hard all year round doing all sorts of things amassing funds to take the lads a drink down. One year he told me the lads were curious about the woman who helped raise so much money for them and he invited me to go along and having filled the boot of my car with several hundred pounds worth of stock, we spent the day down there with the men. You name it and we took it; every drink known to man, every box and bar of chocolate, fancy biscuits, cigarettes and tobacco.

We spent a long day with the lads and they loved it, but as we were about to leave one nurse took me aside and asked were we aware of the bother it caused them? I was astonished, all we were doing was showing the men we remembered their great sacrifice during the Second World War but she told me the men all got so wildly drunk that it was impossible to manage them when we had gone. The aftermath would mean all the staff would have a sleepless night as the nurses had to change their beds, a lot of the men would be ill, they would all have hang overs the next day and in graphic detail she painted a not very pretty picture of the next forty eight hours. Ooops. She'd got more than a point. By now, I was the weekend resident singer compere at the Manor club in West Bridgford and began collecting for them there too, sending a big bucket round and asking the audience for the loose pennies in their pockets but I never went down to show my face on that Blackpool booze run ever again.

The Manor club in it's hey day was a good night out and I quite enjoyed the job. We had a few well known artistes appear there and we also did good trade with our open mike policy that attracted a lot of singers from near and far and although they were amateurs, some of them were the 'walk over hot coals to hear' good. They never came with two names, just Rose, a couple of John's, Dave's and Mick's.... I well recall one chap Barry(?) who used to come regularly every Sunday night. Once seen never forgotten. The first time I saw and heard him I stood rooted to the spot. He sang the Old Rugged Cross, his voice crystal clear and with a truly beautiful resonance but a hymn,? in a *pub*? Then he got to the part of the refrain 'but I'll cherish the old rugged cross' and he took off disco style stamping a heavy rhythm with his feet and bought the roof down. He was wonderful.

One night I was told I had to come in on a mid week and compere a strip show. Ohhh, I was not happy and when I realised it was a MALE strip show, I was even more unhappy. I tried to get out of it but no matter, I was told I cannot just pick and choose I was either the club compere or not. Reluctantly I did it. The first act did his show and I simply stayed in the dressing room out of the way. The second act went out and he worked the audience from one end of the club to the other, and it was a big room packed with the ladies. I peeped through the curtains and waited until he was right at the back of the room before I made for the bar which was close to the stage, to get a much needed drink. He spotted me and made a run for me. I took off like a bat out of hell and nearly took two eight feet wide solid oak doors off their hinges, dived in the loo and locked the door. Not on your Nelly mate and not on your belly mate either.

I saw a change of manager a couple of times whilst I was there and on the last occasion was asked by the outgoing chap an Irish man and his wife who were heading for a pub in Leeds, to come in at the lunch time and be there to welcome the new folks with a cup of tea, something I was more than happy to do as he and his wife had been good folks to work for. On the appointed mid week day, he gave me some last minute instructions along the lines of sending on anything they may have missed and I waved them off and hung around.

I didn't have long to wait as the delivery van arrived first and began off loading the new manager's stuff. I gave them the message to put anything they found onto the van and take it back to Leeds for the outgoing incumbent. The move went smoothly with the new folks arriving some half an hour later. I did the tea and biscuits thing for them and the removal men and then took my leave as I was due back there that night to introduce a special artiste Dean Friedman ('Did You See Lisa?') I arrived at the club that night about 7pm to find the artiste frantically looking for his piano! It was found on the back of a removal van in Leeds! Nowt to do with me!

The eighties were a good time for extra work and Peak Practice was nice to work on while it lasted. Over a couple of years I did quite a few days on it and the various locations took us to some breathtakingly beautiful places like Crich, Whatstandwell, Buxton and Matlock amongst others. But one place I recall was way out in the wilds. They took us by coach to a field and then we had to tramp three quarters of a mile through thick mud to the very edge of a steep cliff and I mean steep enough to require one to bungee jump down its muddy face with the aid of a strategically placed rope one end of which was tied to a stout oak tree! There was a safer but much longer and indirect route through a farmyard but already two jeeps were stuck fast in its mud and though I contemplated this alternative, one look at a lane full of slipping cows kind of put me off.

Coming down was bad enough but don't forget we had to return the same way! I made it down in one piece just and then stood and watched in astonishment as Charlie Bartle who was in his eighties by then shinned down that rope like a good 'un! At the bottom of the 'cliff' was a rocky area with a few caves and the episode concerned some children who were lost and/or injured in there. We were supposedly worried relatives who had to scramble down the steep scree in a driving rain storm in an effort to reach our kids. And the rain?...you got it! The good old hosepipe again!

Out that way too in a house called Wingfield Manor was the setting used for the Chronicles of Narnia in the late 80's. I played a school teacher who had to stop a group of giggling kids and tell them off for their dishevelled appearance. It was a lovely old house with dozens of rooms but it was in serious need of repair. I had the pleasure of meeting and talking to the elderly owners who invited me into their sitting room and as we chatted they told me that TV and film production companies regularly paid a lot of money to use their house on this and other films including Nanny and Jane Eyre. It meant they could do the essential repairs. I asked the old lady how many rooms were in her house, a house in which she had been born and had lived all her life I might add and she told me she didn't know and had never even counted them! Wow, just imagine that.

One day to my surprise, Central TV phoned me direct and asked me if I could help out one of their actors who was coming down from the north to do a couple of days work and needed somewhere to stay overnight. This man was a character actor and although I knew him by sight through his work, I didn't actually *know* him but I agreed to help out. He would be at my place by 8pm at the latest I was told. He turned up at gone midnight and smelled strongly of drink but wasn't in a falling about drunken state I hasten to add. I suspected he'd taken a little refreshment at the studio bar run by Peter Laurie.

My guest was about late 50's early 60's and was as stout as he was tall with double chins falling and melting into spare tyres round his rotund stomach. He had a Friar like bald patch and what hair he had left was long and hung lank like rats tails over his collar, and he wore thick horn rimmed glasses like the bottom of milk bottles. I made him a sandwich and a cup of tea, sat and talked a while as he ate, then showed him to his room. He told me he was worried he would sleep in and miss his call so I assured him I would wake him well in time. He was expecting a taxi at 7am and I would call him at 6.

The next morning dawned with beautiful warm sunshine and I knocked on his door at the appointed time. No answer. I knocked again. My stomach started to churn as there was still no answer. I thought of his over large size and had a vision of him having had a heart attack. After repeated loud knocking, I took my courage in my hands and opened the door. It had been a warm sticky night and he had kicked the quilt off the bed, was lying on his left side with his back to me and with his right leg pulled up high as if in a running position. But it was his night attire I could not take my eyes

233

off. He was sound asleep, snoring gently, his jaw slack and wet and he was wearing a shocking pink lace bra and matching French knickers, with the latter having a sexy split up the side to the waist.

I closed the door hurriedly but quietly and stood there not quite knowing what to do next. The only thing I was sure about was that he had to be woken up. I decided the best thing to do was to shout real loud through the closed door and make a big noise opening it to wake him. As I went in he had just grabbed the quilt and was pulling it into place. After his ablutions, he joined me for breakfast and I made some pleasant small talk. The taxi turned up at a little before 7am and he left. By 7.15am I had called everyone I knew from Lands End to John o' Groats!

"Hello? Oh I am so sorry, did I get you out of bed? Oh just wait'll you 'ear what ah got ter tell ya....."

CHAPTER NINETEEN

WEDDINGS AND FUNERALS

I have concentrated more on the working aspect of my life up to this point but essentially I am first and foremost a family woman and I would now like to tell you how my family life has fared over the last twenty odd years;

My first marriage had died the death the night I have previously told you about, on that fateful winter night. Oh we lingered on for another year or two but I had no faith or expectation that it would get any better. We both wanted different things out of life. At one point knowing how much I hated our house, he thought it might be a good idea to buy us one but nothing came of it. I don't want to and am not going to drag him down into any sort of mud, suffice to say, it was over. (He has never seen his children since they were 9 and 6. His choice.) In November 1969 I finally left him for another man whom I married a few years later. We were to be together for over 22 years but in later years it was to prove to be the worst day's work I had ever done.

We bought a family house in Colwick and I am still here to this day. To say I loved my second husband is not going anywhere near the depth of feelings I had for him. I worshipped the very ground he walked on. I had been warned that after my cone biopsy operation in 1965, any future children I might have would have to be born by C section and in 1971 I gave birth to my last child, our daughter Zoe. I very nearly lost my life with a pulmonary thrombosis which is a special risk associated with having a caesarean.

In the early 70's my 2nd husband's father died. I had loved him to bits and did a lot with and for him. His funeral was an amazing sight. He'd died without a penny in his pocket yet afterwards, thrown on the floor to rot by dozens of his well intentioned fellow Burton Joyce neighbours and friends were literally hundreds of pounds worth of flowers. I thought bitterly of all he could have done with that money but here they were in all there exquisite beauty decaying on the floor at my feet. As soon as the funeral was over, I left and went straight down the 'Green' to see my dad.

He was unusually sat in the front room. I went in, burst into tears and told him of my anger and despair at the waste of all that money spent on those flowers. He went off to make me a cup of tea whilst I pulled myself together. I pressed a ten pound note in his hands (a tidy sum in those day,) and told him this was his flower money, that I was not going to buy him a wreath and told him to go buy himself a pair of trousers – he neither smoked nor drank – told him how much I had appreciated all he had done for me over the years and told him I loved him. He answered that he loved me too....and I am sure he did.

We lost him in Jan 2nd 1977 aged 68 having had both my parents over to spend Boxing Day with us. I bought him a wreath. His death hit me hard and for a while my world fell apart. He was always terrified of dying but he'd simply sat in his chair that Sunday evening opposite my mother and slipped quietly and instantly away, as Mickey his oldest son was to do in March of 2009. I don't know if it was the loss of dad or her restless spirit that made mam move houses a few more times and I continued to do as much for her as I could, once paying for a new carpet for her lounge in yet another of her house moves. But it was like beating my head against a brick wall to get anything back from her and I eventually gave up trying.

In 1980 Laura had married in haste (she was not pregnant) at the tender age of 18 and within six weeks, she told me later, had realised it had been a mistake. She gainfully struggled with it for a few years but she eventually left him. A few years down the divorced line, she was to find true happiness in her soul mate, a Newcastle lad by the name of Paul Hughes and he has truly been a knight in shining Armour to her. Laura is childless by choice. She made up her mind a long time ago not to have children and while on the one hand, I was disappointed since she is a caring person and would have made a good mum, I also admired her honesty when she told me her reasons. I have to tell you that skinny little baby of mine lost both her breasts seven years ago and is now punching the air in her battle for her life over bone cancer and Paul has been her stalwart. I can never find the words to tell her how courageous I think she is and how important I think he is to all of us.

Cindy was next to do the trip up the aisle, having 'courted' for a good few years. Her beau was nothing if not sporty and was captain of the football team, the cricket team etc. Cindy more or less put her life on hold as she helped support his efforts until he'd finished his education. I'm positive all mum's and maybe some dad's too who are reading this book will agree with me when I say it's not easy giving your kids up. Her husband the flame haired Keith Pickering is the best in the world and I wanted her happiness more than anything but ohhhh it hurt so much more to let her go and I still don't understand why. I had trouble letting Laura go for obvious reasons and Zoe because she was the last and the baby of the family, but nothing like this.

Because of my attachment to her, Cindy's planned 1986 May wedding was not going to be the joyous occasion it should have been for me. I was going to miss her something cruel. My husband knew it too. She is tiny, petite and looked wonderful in her fairy tale white gown and breaking with tradition strolled round in all her wedding finery to the village church a couple of hundred yards away. She proudly walked down the aisle on her 'dad's' arm as I had done so many years before. I managed to keep a stiff upper lip but nearly lost it when my husband made a speech at the reception and told the guests how much I would miss her, but taking a chunk out of my bottom lip to the point of blood kept the tears back.

The newly weds very sensibly I thought, decided to go away on honeymoon directly from the reception and so there was no long hoot nanny to go through with its inevitable early morning drunken anti climax. But I had reckoned without our guests. After we had waved them off, we came home followed by a whole lot of them who were hell bent on having the reception continued at our house. When we got here, I took my husband to one side on his own in the kitchen and said quietly;
"You know where I am going, you know what I am going to do, and so just keep every one away from me whilst I do it will you?"

I just about made it to our bedroom, closed the door and threw back the quilt intending to bury my head into the pillows and let go the torrent of tears I had managed to hold back all day. On my pillow was a white envelope addressed to 'Mum' and inside was the most beautiful letter. It is one of my most precious possessions and reads;

238

Mum,

   Well as one door closes, another one opens. I look back through the closing door and I see years of caring, crying, loving, sharing, fun and happiness. I see endless summer holidays, magical Christmases. The memories are so important. They mean so much to me – you mean so much to me.

   As I look through the new door I see a life as filled with love as it has always been. I see Keith loving me and, one day, children. I am on the threshold of something new and exciting.

   You've been a good teacher and a loving mother. You've given your life for us and I appreciate all you've done.

I hope you were proud today.

I love you, sleep tight.

Cindy
xxx

Mum,

Well as one door closes, another one open
I look back through the closing door and
I see years of caring, crying, loving, sharing,
fun, and happiness. I see endless summer
holidays, magical christmases. The memories
are so important. They mean so much to me —
You mean so much to me.

As I look through the new door I see a
life as filled with love as it has always
been. I see Keith loving me and, one day,
children. I am on the threshold of something
new and exciting.

You've been a good teacher and a loving
mother. You've given your life for us and
I appreciate all you've done.

I hope that you were proud today.

I love you, Sleep tight.

Cindy.
x x o

Now the floodgates opened and how.......

240

In 1988 Keith who was working for Cooper - Lybrand Accountants at that time, got the chance to work abroad for a while. He naturally discussed it with his wife. He excitedly talked of maybe going to Australia and painted a rosy picture of watching England play cricket there.

"No, let's go to Hong Kong."

"Or, I know, how about Barbados or the Bahamas! Imagine rolling out of bed in the morning and running straight into the ocean..."

"Let's go to Hong Kong."

"Or maybe we could even go to Canada, we could learn to ski.."

"Hong Kong."

"What's the fascination with Hong Kong?"

"It's the only place in the world that mum wants to go."

And she was right. I was fascinated with it and the idea that I would one day visit that place had been born when I was very young. Back in the forties, everything we owned as children whether it be toys, plimsolls, books or clothing, somewhere on it would be the legend Made in Hong Kong. The more I saw those words, the more I yearned to see it. So Hong Kong it was. The idea of them going all that way and for all that time was horrendous to me but in due time, they rented their house out and set off to a new life for a few years.

Her almost daily letters began arriving within days. Her narratives were so descriptive I felt as if I had already been there and could almost smell the very air she was breathing. They were long and full of the excitement of living there and through them, as I gleaned many strange place names like Kowloon, Lantau, Chung Chau, Silver Bay, Peng Chau, Aberdeen Harbour, and of course the fabulous shopping in

Stanley Market, little did I know that one day I too would walk in her footsteps and visit all these enchanting places.

Then a letter came one day that was just as long and chatty as all the others. It was full of the joys of their busy Hong Kong life, their work, the many new ex pat friends they had made, the shopping and dining out. So why did it give me cause for concern? It was that odd feeling again, the same one I'd had when my young brother had been taken into hospital a little after I had got married. I began to pace up and down and I just knew something was wrong. After a few hours of wearing the carpet out and neither knowing nor caring what time it was over there, I picked up the phone and rang her.

She answered and I said;

"It's me....mum. What's wrong?"

Her answer was lost in floods of tears. She hated her job, hated Hong Kong and longed to be home.

It took her quite a while to settle but settle she eventually did after finding a job she loved and I went out twice to spend time there. I adored it. The first time was in the wake of my recent marriage break up. It had only been a mere few weeks before and she invited me to go out to her for Christmas. Like I was going to say no! I was not looking forward to Christmas at home and so focused on my coming trip.

She had warned me not to take too many clothes as there were hundreds of factory shops that sold designer gear for pennies and it proved to be the case. But my suitcase wasn't empty; it was packed to the very gills with Christmas gifts for them from family and friends. As I'd prepared for the trip, I offered to take her whatever stuff she wanted me to bring from home and what she asked for was to confound the people who unusually checked my suitcase at the Heathrow check in. The staff were bemused and amazed when they sifted through my *belongings and found dozens of packets of the much loved Bachelors Savoury Rice Cindy had asked for!*

Those festively wrapped gifts were to prove a real worry to the airline staff. Did I know what was in them? No I didn't. Did I know the people who had given them to me? Yes I did, they were family and friends. Still they demurred and I told them that sooner than have them worry, I would open them all up here and now and re-wrap them when I got to Hong Kong. Only then did they let me go with my packages intact. I found out afterwards, there had been a bomb scare and that's what this had all been about.

Hong Kong proved to me to be all I had expected and more than I had imagined. Whilst the kids were at work I spent every day exploring strange places. I got on ferries with no idea where I was going (the writings all Greek to me!) and landed up in some odd little villages where time had really stopped. On one trip to Peng Chau I inadvertently missed the last ferry and stood for some considerable time alone as the day darkened into night. A small boat rowed by a man pulled up and asked what I was doing. I told him I was waiting for the ferry.

"No ferry, ferry finished, ferry gone."

By descriptive hand motions and pointing I got the impression he was offering to take me to the next island that had a ferry still running and I jumped at the chance not liking the idea of spending the night on the jetty! He kindly rowed me across the bay and I gave him a few dollars which he smilingly took.

The whole Hong Kong experience was idyllic and more than lived up to my expectations, though now and again I desperately needed a sleeve to tug on if only to say 'Look at that....'. One day she took me to the top of the Victoria Peak, on Austin Mountain, one of the most famous views in the entire world. She tried to prepare me for it, describing it to me over and over again but I defy anyone not to break out in king sized goose bumps when they round that corner and get their first glimpse through the tree's of the bay below. Not much silences me but that did. Every precious second of that day is welded into my heart.

They came back after a couple of years to begin their family and went on to have my two lovely granddaughters for whom the hiccup of history has struck in that Phoebe is like her Aunty Laura, a tomboy character and sports mad, whilst Hattie is the spit from her own mother's mouth being utterly girly and feminine. The years have slipped quickly away and I believe Cindy and Keith are due to celebrate their silver wedding anniversary next year.

Some years after Cindy's wedding and a month after Zoe my youngest daughter married, I got a special letter from her also. This too is a heartbreaker but runs to many pages and is far too personal to include here. Suffice to say I hold it just as dear to my heart. She went on to marry twice. Alan her second husband is a property developer. He's a good hard working man, a good husband and father who took to Joseph like he was his own. She has given me three grandsons; Joseph Jack who shows signs of great talent and has designs on a musical career, Sam Jack who is incredibly handsome and should be modelling and baby Toby Jack who is, to our utter relief, now showing great promise after a worrying start to his life.

1989 also proved to be memorable for three reasons; my mother's death, the end of my marriage and the last vestige of Salvation Army indoctrinated belief in God was irrevocably stripped away never to return. When mam died aged 70, I hold my hand up to the fact that I didn't want to go to her funeral as we had been estranged for a couple of years but out of *genuine consideration for my siblings, I went. Mickey didn't, he had no shoes he said. Its always been a wonder to me just how many hundreds if not thousands of people we meet throughout our lives; friends and acquaintances, relatives, work colleagues, maybe even folk we meet and chat to on a regular basis in the street, the doctors surgery or on the bus and yet when we kick the bucket how relatively few people actually attend our funerals. And talking of which, although I still hate the idea of all those flowers being wasted at funerals, I have been to one that asked for donations to charity in lieu of flowers and it was a grim colourless affair and lets not even talk about the graveside burial I attended, they are **truly** horrible.*

The most important thing in life to me was not my kids, not my husband, not my work, not our house, not me. It was and always had been my marriage because that was the basic cement that held everything else so beautifully together. Everyone who knew us held us up as living proof that marriage can work and we were the rare sort of people who gave it a good name. I worked really hard on it, supported him fully in everything he wanted to do. I saw it as laying gold – above and beyond the call of duty - bricks down to make and hold the foundations.

In 1972 we moved to London in pursuit of my husbands efforts to resume his chosen career as a police officer. (Back then in 1968, the constabulary was very moralistic and he'd been forced to resign because of his affair with me. Yet we knew of many other policemen who did exactly the same but kept it quiet and they got away with it.) After we were married 4 years later, he applied to rejoin the police force but was turned down. Now he applied to the Derbyshire constabulary and finally, in an every widening search, even the

245

Leicestershire force turned him down. I did all I could to help him achieve his ambitions and after watching the light of hope die in his eyes after each rejection, I finally wrote to the Home Office and asked for their advice. Their reply was short and sweet; get him down here, there is a job waiting for him. There was no hesitation; we made plans to leave for London even going so far as to rent our beloved home out to a Dr Jekyll and his family.

('I have heard every joke about my name ma-am twice over, every darned one of 'em!')

My husband had to go first and undertake a few months of re-training. There was no accommodation for families until such time as this training was complete and having given up our house, me and our kids lived in limbo and threw ourselves upon first my sister Sandra in her tiny house and then my good friend Sheila in Leeds. I repeat; beloved sister, or good friend, 'guests and wet fish begin to stink after 5 days!'

We finally moved down to London, lock stock and three kids just in time for Christmas 1972 when his re-training was completed. Our accommodation was a flat on St Germans Road, in Forest Hill. It was on the third floor of a concrete block, was cold and damp with a vista of a gasometer amongst a million rooftops and chimney pots and we lived with little comfort having let our house out in Colwick fully furnished. We had a new car which cost us a fortune in repayments and running costs but he worked several miles away across London and needed it himself so what with no transport and three kids, I could not work and so was unable to help financially.

I had a love hate relationship with London. I didn't like it. It's an exciting city true and we got to do lots of things down there - provided it didn't cost too much of course. But London

246

always was the most expensive place to live. Even back then; where a cinema ticket cost about £2 here in Nottingham, there it was a massive £7! But there were things to do down there like be on the front row of the Mall when all the pomp and pageantry of Princess Annes' wedding procession went past, but essentially it's one giant transit camp of strangers and is on the move day and night like an ultra sophisticated ant heap.

The rate of inflation at that time was to soar scandalously high and having let the house and set the rent to cover our mortgage, we suddenly found ourselves in deep trouble as the interest rate soared and we had to subsidise our tenants. When he had been forced to retire from his police job, he'd been given his considerable pension pot back and now that had to be re-paid as well and they took it at a swingeing rate. We lived in penury but I thought it worth it as I took pride in watching him find his own feet again after more than three years on and off the dole and in and out of jobs he had no love for. I am a firm believer that you do a job you love that only seems like eight hours a day rather than one you hate that seems like sixteen.

Poverty was not new to me but it was a whole lot different with three dependant children. I learned how to bone and stuff a pigs head for Sunday lunch and make a good meal out of it, (stop wincing, it's delicious.) There was a charity shop just around the corner and with the help of my trusty old sewing machine I was able to keep us all reasonably well dressed for pennies. One morning I took a bag of old clothes there. It was closed but a note on the door said to leave any donations round the back. I went round and found a like bag of clothing left on the doorstep. It was full of quality men's shirts and jumpers. I swapped the bags. He was as badly off for decent clothes as we were. Trust me, I have more than made up for it since and regularly pass on all my clothing and household linen to charity shops.

One day Cindy came home from school all excited. There was to be a boat trip from school along the Thames. She was so thrilled at the idea and of course it was out of the question that she did not go. She HAD to go. I shouldn't think it was more than a couple of quid at the most but it took some finding. She was to take a packed lunch and a small amount of money to buy a drink. She went off in high spirits and then went all day long without a drink just so she could bring home that shilling (5p). What a kid.

At Cindy's school I met a lovely young woman named Shirley. She had four small children and her hubby had walked out and left them all. She was so pretty, with a slim trim figure; one of those delicate fragile women whom men seem to want to cherish usually. She had taken the rejection really badly and ended up in a psychiatric hospital after trying to kill herself. She dreamed of meeting THE man who would come along on the proverbial white charger. We became firm friends and one day she asked me if I would be offended if she gave me some clothes for toddler Zoe. Poor little soul was the worst dressed of all of us because she grew so fast and was still wearing baby stuff she'd grown out of months ago so I jumped at the chance. The clothing she gave me and it was a vast amount, was exquisite. I didn't have to buy her anything at all for about a year or more. When we moved back I lost touch with Shirley and through the years I have often thought of her and sent her love, thanks and silent good wishes for a man on a white charger.....

In the early 70's London was awash with all the people expelled from Uganda by Idi Amin and Cindy found herself in

248

a class which was predominantly non English speaking. She had been doing so well at school in Colwick but in the rush to get those children speaking English, she was largely left to her own devices and her education began to slip badly. I went to the school and saw her teacher and told her of my worries. Instead of the sympathy and constructive advice I expected to get, she unloaded all her troubles about teaching the immigrants when they did not even understand her and merely suggested I get some books out of the library for her to read. In despair I wrote to Miss Custerson back home at St John the Baptist School in Colwick Nottingham and by return of post, got reams of advice and lists of books for home teaching.

St German's Road had once been a truly beautiful street of impressive elegant three storey houses with grandiose columned fronts and massive tennis court sized back gardens. Then the developers moved in. Each time a house became empty, the wreckers came along and with one of those huge balls smashed straight through it, roof to basement, in order to stop squatters moving in. Then it was left in his appallingly dangerous condition, with tons of rubble and heaps of broken glass. It could stay like this for a matter of days or a couple of years before the site was cleared I was told by my neighbours, then a couple of blocks of soulless flats would eventually be thrown up. There were several such houses thus destroyed and they were dangerous and an eyesore.

Zoe was by now a toddler with long white blonde hair that gleamed in the sunshine and she was incredibly curious. Amidst all the chaos there was on that road, she went missing. One second she was playing in the huge back garden of our flat and the next there was no sight of her. Calling and increasingly screaming her name Laura, Cindy and I went looking for her, my imagination doing its bloodiest worse. At each demolished house, we clambered over the rubble, trying to avoid broken piping and jagged glass, all the while frantically calling her name.

In some houses the staircases still stood but led nowhere and I had a horrible vision of her chubby little legs climbing up them and falling to her death in what was left of the basement. I prayed to a God I no longer believe in to give her back to me and I would lay my life at his feet and never say a cross word to her ever again. Having got to the end of the road we crossed over and began to search the opposite side my mind now working overtime on paedophiles. By now I was in floods of tears and felt terrified, hopeless, helpless and abandoned.

Finally, two doors away from where we lived was an old peoples place and an old lady opened up her window and asked were we looking for a little girl. She told us she was in her back garden picking blackberries. As we went down the side of the house, she was coming to meet us, her little face hands and dress soaked in the purple juice. I didn't know whether to shout at her, hug her or slap her, I did all three!

And so I unhappily penny pinched my way through our time in London and in retrospect I am justifiably proud of the way I managed. I ached for the day we could return home though and regular as clockwork and every chance we got, we high tailed it back to Nottingham. Here I would like to pay tribute to my sister Sandra and my brother-in-law John Aston. At that time they lived in a tiny cramped semi det council house in Aspley with their three small children but throughout our time down there, she was the only one who held out her hand and helped us, putting us up every single time without demur and never once making us feel anything less than welcome. I would like to take this opportunity to say I owe them a huge debt of gratitude and I thank them both once more.

It was to be nigh on three years later we moved back and I had a handful of truly good happily married years. Gradually though and despite my very best efforts it fell apart and after several years I found the strength to finally let him go. I had to. I asked him to leave the family home in September 1989, the day before my fiftieth birthday, which he did. It was a few weeks later at that dreaded 1989 Christmas that I flew to Hong Kong! It took me a long long time to get over my marriage break-up, to stop caring but eventually time really does heal. Twenty years on to the very day I am now happier than I have been in donkeys years and I would not swap my 'now' life with anyone.

Oh how the world has changed in my short span of time and to me, it does seem a short span. Our generation are what time, tide, experience and circumstance have made of us. The unkempt ragged kids a lot of us once were are now old and dare I say in some cases fragile, yet despite that sometimes frailty, we are still capable of coherent thought and innovative ideas. Discussing the increasing traffic problems with my family one day, I said the time would come in the not too distant future when a brave government would have to put a limit on just who should be allowed to drive and my kids laughed at me.

But stop and think about it; the British School of Motoring boasts they pass someone every ten minutes, that's just one driving school, how many thousands of other driving schools are there on this crowded island of ours and how many drivers seeking our blessed asylum are adding to it daily? My eldest daughter said that as old people die off, it levels itself *out. That's ludicrous. Never in history of the world has man lived longer than he does today.*

Traffic increases hourly and we cannot simply magic land to build the roads for it to run on. Governments need to be brave and build an infrastructure that is accessible to every single person from one end of this land to the other and they should have made a start in that direction many years ago, they most certainly need to start right now. Oh yes, we may creak a bit but we oldies are still capable of imaginative thought, or isn't that merely using the common sense we were born with?

I left school at fifteen with no qualifications. Now, who'd have thought I, who failed my eleven plus so miserably, would ever have mastered something as complex as a computer, certainly not me. Something John Holmes said when he interviewed me and reviewed 'Yo'd Mek a Parson Swear....Again!' on BBC Radio Nottingham a few weeks ago, made me think. He told me I looked younger than my years. (Oh I agree...I look in the mirror at my wrinkle free face and marvel at it. See? There IS some compensation for getting old; you lose your sharp eyesight! And I have heard it said; a man is responsible for every wrinkle on a woman's face, a child for every grey hair! I don't have grey hair either and my kids can look through my bathroom cupboards and drawers till the cows come home and they will not find hair dye! It's in the kitchen hidden behind the cereal boxes! *) But no matter what I look like there's no getting away from those infernal numbers.*

John Holmes thought it amazing to sit down and write a book at my age and I passed comment that although he is not as old as I am, he is in a predominantly youthful occupation yet he too is still doing a wonderful job of his show after so

252

many years. (And if you haven't caught his programme you really should, the man takes on anything!) He paused for a second and then said he thought we still had a lot of fire left in our bellies and were a generation that would not willingly lie down and wait to die. He is right. Have you taken a look at the age of a lot of the assistants sat at supermarket tills these days? It's quite an eye opener. Some of these oldies have been forced back into work by the wanton waste and outright theft of their pensions by this blasted government, but some actually CHOOSE to carry on working.

Our generation will not lightly give up on our jobs, our homes, our hopes and dreams for a future we still want to be part of, simply because those numbers dictate we should.

We will not willingly give up on our hobbies like dancing - though our bingo wings seem to have a rhythm of their own these days - we'll not readily give up on our driving or swimming, walking, running and dare I say it, for some oldies the one thing we are good at and what we have perfected through years of experience, our sex life. There, that's shocked you hasn't it?

I recently joined the gym. You should just see the place. It's magnificent all marble and chrome and off peak you see a lot of us creaking oldies keeping fit on machines just a dot away from the examples of torture racks in museums. There are miles of wrinkled skin pushed into tight stretchy Lycra in gaudy colours, skinny vests, head bands, wrist sweat bands and top of the range flashy trainers....and that's just the men! They like me will neither slow down nor lie down whilst waiting to drop off the perch simply because those biblical three score years and ten, which are just ten days away for me now, tell us we ought to.

There are still occasions when I long for that 'sleeve to tug on' but as time goes on, that's become increasingly unlikely, though I continue to pull my stomach in just on the off chance – my idea of being shot by a younger jealous wife on my 90th birthday still remains a possibility!

I consider myself very lucky; I have some amazing true friends – male and female - the friendship of which in some cases has been donkey's years in the making and proving. As I have grown older I have become kinder and less critical of myself and dare I hope, of others. I have come to the conclusion, that like most things in life, others do this hatchet job so much better than me anyway. I am entitled to a treat now and again so I don't begrudge myself the odd cream cake, well not much. I am becoming my own best friend and decided long ago to adopt the Bill Oddie style of housekeeping. This means I just don't notice dust anymore and not making my bed is no longer the big deal I once thought it to be.

I have a neat little trick I'd like to pass on to like minded people: always prop several prominent 'get well soon' cards on the mantelpiece then if unexpected guests arrive, they'll think you've been sick and unable to clean. I've known some folk be so fooled into feeling sorry for me they've pulled on my strategically 'left lying on the work top' marigolds and done all the, cleaning and washing up for me!

I have sadly seen a good few of my friends leave this world far too soon before they really understood the great freedom and wisdom that comes with old age. Whose business is it but mine if I choose to read or play on the computer until 4am and go to bed at 9pm or even vice versa? I will still jig to those wonderful tunes of the 60's & 70's and if at the same time I wish to weep over a lost love or two, I will...although latter day knowledge tells me the boot might be on the other foot these days.

With the exception of the age of 10, every birthday that tripped into another decade has been painful to me and as I have reached each and every one of them I have thought longingly of the decade I have just moved out of aware of how I hated going into it and at the moment I am keenly aware that this is the last Saturday of my 60's! The same applies to my figure, the one I have and hate today, will be the one I wish I had tomorrow.....

*It's a cliché to say to say 'you can't put an old head on young shoulders' but you can never destroy the child in the adult either and the two of us have walked hand in hand through the decades of life into old age. I have to admire the little girl in me. Some stubborn streak in her made her refuse to roll over, made her haul herself up and out by her bootlaces and stride forward to better things...and she did. My dad used to say to me I had to learn that there **are** such words as 'it can't be done'. Dad, you were wrong. Oh yes it can be done no matter what it is. If the will is there, then anything can be achieved, that little girl in me still says all it needs is the will and above all she was wilful.*

*The old woman in me feels fit and my mind is crystal clear as I write this and like I've said before, I aint done yet! I intend to buy what I want; two of if I want, pay what I want for it, when I want, go where I want and do what I want as often as I want, since happily there is no-one to tell me I can't anymore. I intend to continue to be messy, disorganised, unobservant, woolly headed, argumentative and extravagant; in fact I intend to finally just be **ME**!*

Life is wonderful and it sure as hell beats the alternative....and, having rather belatedly found I seem to have the gift for writing, I intend to carry on as long as there's lead in me pencil!

THE END